THE ENIGMA
OF REINCARNATION

by

BRAD STEIGER

ACE BOOKS, INC.
1120 Avenue of the Americas
New York, N.Y. 10036

The Author wishes to express his sincere thanks to those who donated so generously of their time, their talent, and their knowledge in the preparation of this book.

An *ACE STAR* BOOK by arrangement with the Author

Printed in the U.S.A.

Have you ever walked down a street in a strange city and been overwhelmed with the sudden familiarity of it? Have you ever seemed to experience the arousal of some long-forgotten memory when you lay at ease, completely tranquil?

● ● ● ●

I do, I feel, have an open mind, and I do believe in the existence of spiritual man, but my entire intellectual, emotional and religious bias is against reincarnation.

Why should a man choose to write a book on a subject toward which he has long held prejudgement?

. . . Because of an irritating number of cases that cry out in very articulate and demanding voices to be more carefully studied.

. . . Because of case histories that hold up under the most exacting examination.

. . . Because of the impressive number of great minds who, through the ages, have professed their acceptance of reincarnation as a reality.

. . . Because, and for this reason most of all, I, like so many others, have had those strange, illusory glimpses of what seems to be a past life. . . .

From the Introduction,
by Brad Steiger

By the Author*

TREASURE HUNTING   (K-268)
STRANGE GUESTS   (K-241)

*Available in ACE STAR edition

CONTENTS

INTRODUCTION—REINCARNATION:
  FACT OR FANTASY?   7

REMEMBRANCES OF LIVES PAST   17

"THEM DAMN YANKEES SHOT ME"   35

BRIDEY MURPHY REVISITED   51

REINCARNATION—OR A VOICE FROM BEYOND?   61

A MOST UNUSUAL FAMILY   75

THE MYSTERY OF NAOMI HENRY   80

WHOSE HAND GUIDED THE PAINTBRUSH?   88

THE MURDERED MAN AND THE TEENAGE GIRL   91

CAN WE REMEMBER OUR ANCESTORS' LIVES?   95

PAUL TWITCHELL—THIS GENERATION'S
  EDGAR CAYCE   105

THE MAN WHO RETURNED AS HIS GRANDSON   126

BACK TO MOTHER'S ARMS   131

EAST IS EAST AND WEST IS WEST   136

"DON'T CALL ME ISMAIL!"   140

THE THIRD TIME AROUND   143

THE EXECUTIONER LEFT HIS MARK   146

DOES THIS BOY PROVE REINCARNATION?   149

RETURN OF THE MURDERED HEIR   153

THE PAST LIFE OF BHAJAN SINGH   156

THE POISON VICTIM CAME BACK   161

REINCARNATION AND ESP   164

THE MAN WHO IS HIS OWN UNCLE   173

THE CASE FOR REINCARNATION   177

INTRODUCTION

REINCARNATION: FACT OR FANTASY?

"I have always had this very strange recurring dream. I see myself as a cowboy during a trail drive. It seems like it must be sometime after the Civil War because some of the men have on battered military hats and high cavalry boots. There is an argument about whether the men should rustle the herd from the owner. I defend the rancher, tell the men that they're crazy to think of stealing. I talk too much. One of the men pulls a revolver and shoots me in the chest. And it is all so real! I can feel that slug burn; I can smell gunpowder and cattle; I can see jagged streaks of lightning scratching the dark sky; I can hear the excited chatter of the men get farther and farther away as I lie there dying. Then I wake up, but it has all been so real! Am I actually remembering how I died in a former life?"

❋ ❋ ❋ ❋

"My husband and I went to Mexico last summer. It was something that I had always wanted to do, ever since I was just a little girl. We saw all the things *touristas* are supposed to see; then, on a peculiar compulsion, I asked my husband to turn off on a sideroad.

We had been strongly advised to keep to the main routes, but I had an unquenchable desire to take this particular road. After we had driven a few miles, we came to an obscure little village. It was dirty, unattractive, but I *knew* that village. It sounds crazy to say it, but I felt that I had lived there before. I knew the arrangement of the town square; I knew the path that led to the lake; and most peculiar of all, I felt a great feeling of warmth toward a withered old couple sunning themselves outside their hut. I actually felt as though they might have been my parents when I lived in that village during a former incarnation."

* * * *

"I don't know if this means I believe in love at first sight or what, but when I first met Sarah, I felt that I had known her before. After we had dated for a while, she admitted that she had experienced the same sort of feeling towards me. Just for fun, we checked all the places we had lived as kids or traveled through on vacation trips, but we had never come within a thousand miles of each other before we met. The weirdest part is that I feel that we've lived together before, maybe as man and wife, maybe as brother and sister. We plan to be married soon. What else can we do? It seems as though we have always been together."

* * * *

Have you, as have my three correspondents quoted above, ever asked yourself, "How many people am I?"

Have you ever walked down a street in a strange city and been overwhelmed with the sudden familiarity of its shop windows, sidewalks, and store fronts?

Have you ever seemed to experience the arousal of

some long-forgotten memory when you lay at ease with a completely tranquil mind? Or has a hidden memory ever been stimulated by witnessing a dramatic re-enactment of some scene from the past?

In my article, "How Many People Are You?" (*Exploring the Unknown*, February, 1963), I related the story of an 18-year-old typist, Miss Dorothy Jordan of Belfast, Ireland, who claimed to have recalled a past life while watching a movie in Liverpool, England.

The theater seemed to become unnaturally dark, and an almost eerie silence enveloped the viewers of *Tudor Rose*, as the condemned Lady Jane Grey was led to the masked executioner.

As Lady Jane bent her head to the chopping block, a hysterical scream pierced the hush. Silhouetted against the screen was a young woman, waving her arms and shouting: "It's all wrong, all wrong! I know; I was at the execution!"

The year was 1936, and even the poorest student of history in the audience could estimate that an eyewitness to the execution of Lady Jane would have to be pushing four hundred!

The distraught girl fell in a faint, and ushers carried her to the lobby. When revived, Dorothy Jordan told a remarkable story to a reporter for the *Empire News*. According to the young typist, she had been transported back to another era while she sat watching the film.

When the screen flashed Lady Jane Grey waving through the tower window to her husband, Lord Guilford Dudley, on his way to his own execution, Miss Jordan realized that this was wrong. She knew the room well, and it was impossible to look out of the window!

It was during the execution scene that she first realized she had been Lady Jane's lady-in-waiting! She saw many things in the movie that did not agree with the facts. She had a vivid impression of the executioner, particularly the broad black bands around his wrists. When Lady Jane first saw him, Miss Jordan recalls that she shuddered and clung to her. Then Lady Jane knelt to the block. They lifted her curls . . . and Miss Jordan saw no more. Apparently she fainted.

When she regained consciousness, the surroundings seemed strange. She was amazed to find herself not in Tudor dress. She is absolutely convinced that the execution happened just as she said.

The reporter from the *Empire News* stated that Miss Jordan appeared to be frank, intelligent, and far from flighty. Upon investigation, it was learned that Miss Jordan had never displayed any particular interest in history and had no knowledge of the various theories of reincarnation.

If we choose to believe the earnest Miss Jordan and the investigation of the *Empire News*, then we will assess this case as an instance in which a young Irishwoman was prompted into reliving the memory of an execution which took place on Tower Hill, London, in 1554.

The whole proposition becomes less laughable if we admit that, at one time or another, we have all felt familiarity in new surroundings, discovered an old house that evoked strange emotions, or had the *deja vu* experience of feeling "that's happened to me before." But is this "sense of the already known," as it is called in parapsychology, reincarnation? Could it not be another manifestation of extrasensory perception, the powers that are man's very own? Could it not be genetic memory, inherited flashes of memories transferred through our ancestors' genes, just like the color of our hair and the size of our brains?

Not too many years ago, a farmer in Wurttemberg, Germany, claimed that he could draw plans of primitive edifices that had been erected on stakes in the marshy Federsee district, many centuries ago.

Taking a bold gamble for orthodox men of science, archeologists began excavations on the basis of the farmer's drawings. It was discovered that the man had hardly missed a thing. Even a hearth marked in one site was exactly where he had indicated that it would be.

When the archeologists returned to question the farmer in order to learn more about the source of his information, the man unhesitatingly told them that he had lived in the primitive lake dwellings during their early habitation.

Reincarnation or genetic memory?

Or what about the actual possession of the living by the dead?

A former Nazi lieutenant, who had been stationed in occupied France during World War II, gave a newspaper this enigmatic personal memoir.

He had received orders to establish quarters in an obscure Rhone valley village. Immediately upon arrival, the lieutenant was seized by the bizarre sensation that this remote village was not so foreign to him after all. As he strolled past a school house, he suddenly had a clear and nostalgic memory of toiling at its cramped wooden desks. In the same puzzling flash of recollection, he remembered his parental home at the back of a small, dingy confectionary shop.

The young German officer traced a boyhood path that lay somewhere in subconscious memory patterns. The elderly woman who opened the creaking door of the shabby house blinked at him in bewilderment as he tried to communicate with the aid of a simplified French-German dictionary.

"There is a small alcove in this house," he managed in his broken French. "It has a small brown cupboard filled with many toys. A small, broken rocking horse stands beside a large stuffed dog. . . ."

The French woman was dumbfounded at first, then

she became a little frightened. How could a German officer, a stranger to their village, describe an upstairs room that he had never seen?

The lieutenant insisted on confirming his description, and trembling with doubt and distrust, the old Frenchwoman led him to the room, where, just as he had said, there stood a cupboard full of toys and a rocking horse near a stuffed dog.

Her eyes glistening with tears, the Frenchwoman told the German officer that 21 years earlier her little nine-year-old son had died. In respect of his memory, she rarely entered the room and had left all of his toys scattered where he had last played with them.

"On what date did your son die?" the young officer asked, his voice trembling with excitement.

"Why," she hesitated, "on February 8th."

"That's my birthday," the lieutenant whispered solemnly.

Had the little French boy been reborn as a German? What strange odyssey had brought the boy back to his home village in the person of an invading officer? Or had the young lieutenant been temporarily possessed by the restless soul of the French boy? In the view of modern parapsychology, something of this sort could have been accomplished by the telepathic reception of a discarnate memory pattern.

There are always plenty of such tales in circulation as that of the young German lieutenant, and some must be taken as embellished or completely imaginary anecdotes conjured up by barroom orators, bored housewives, or "true believers." However, one does occasionally encounter a carefully investigated and thoroughly documented case study of a disturbingly well-founded claim of reincarnation.

This book came into being because of my acquaintance with several cases that seem to be so extensively documented that any error of judgment on the part of the investigators seems completely out of the question.

I have written ten books on such strange and inexplicable phenomena as poltergeists, ghosts, the power of prophecy, and unidentified flying objects. I have prepared dozens of articles on the weird and the unknown for such magazines as *Saga, Family Weekly,* and *Exploring the Unknown.* I am known to the many mediums, faith healers, prophets, and Ufologists whom I have interviewed as a friendly skeptic, and wish to report their stories accurately and objectively. As Long John Nebel said over his radio show in June of 1967, "Brad Steiger has an open mind, but there is certainly no hole in it!"

I do, I feel, have an open mind, and I do believe in the existence of spiritual man (i.e. that man and mind are something other than physical things) but my entire intellectual, emotional, and religious bias is against reincarnation.

The majority of Western man shares my prejudice. A friend of mine, who is an Oriental, once told me that, in his estimation, Western man's refusal to consider the dogma of reincarnation was the major barrier preventing a greater understanding between East and West and a greater harmony between Judeo-Christian theology and the religious doctrines of the Orient.

Why should a man choose to write a book on a subject toward which he has long held a prejudgment?

Because of an irritating number of cases that cry out in very articulate and demanding voices to be more carefully studied.

Because of the case histories that hold up under the most exacting documentation and examination.

Because of the impressive number of great minds who,

through the ages, have professed their acceptance of reincarnation as reality.

Because, and for this reason most of all, I, like so many others, have had those strange, illusory glimpses (could they *really* be memories?) of what seems to be a past life—glimpses so vivid that they must be more than just a drama produced by the brain's dream machinery . . . glimpses so powerful that they must be a product of some as yet unnamed power of subconscious, the reception of telepathic impulses from incarnate or disincarnate beings, the genetically transferred memory of a forgotten ancestor, or yes, a recollection of a past life.

A Swedish scientist, Dr. Lund of Upsala University, has been conducting some remarkable experiments with subjects who claim to remember other lives.

Lund records the case of a 40-year-old woman who, in the presence of witnesses, was hypnotized. While in this state, she was told that she was once again a child. At once the woman behaved in a child-like manner. A demonstration of hypnotically induced age regression is not, of course, at all unique. But when Lund suggested that the woman was once again a baby, the woman altered her actions to fit the role.

Then came the most remarkable aspect of the experiment. Dr. Lund suggested that the woman return to her mother's womb. After a brief hesitation, the woman assumed the position of an embryo.

"Now," Dr. Lund persisted, "what were you five years *before* your birth?"

The woman's normal voice became gruff and hoarse. "It's very hot in here," the voice complained through the agency of the woman.

"What is your name?" asked Dr. Lund.

"Age Karlstrom."

"Your profession?"

"I am a farmer in Mjolbly," she answered gruffly.

"Do you have children?"

"Yes, three."

The woman, in her memory as Age Karlstrom, quickly gave the names of the children and several other details of life on a farm in Mjolbly. Dr. Lund's assistants subsequently investigated the woman's former life and established evidence that a farmer named Age Karlstrom had lived in Mjolbly. Four months before the woman's birth, he had died, leaving the three children whose names he had mentioned during the experiment as his survivors.

Johann Wolfgang Goethe, the great German dramatist and poet, was convinced that the soul inhabited those bodies best fitted to its inherent nature, wandering from one to the other, forcing the flesh to adapt itself without choice. Goethe was a great believer in reincarnation, and he once exclaimed to Charlotte Von Stein that in some previous existence she had been either his sister or his wife.

"The thought of death," Goethe wrote, "leaves me unmoved, since I am convinced that our spirit is indestructible, something which progresses perpetually from infinitude to the endless."

At the very mention of the subject of reincarnation, the cynic ignores the vast amount of empirical evidence and scoffs, refusing even to test the validity of phenomena as yet unrecognized by his science. It would not impair the mental processes of even the most rigid materialist to consider that man may be more than flesh and blood, that the subliminal self may continue to exist without brute matter.

To those who would read this book in an open-minded spirit of inquiry, I can promise a most fascinating series of adventures. Then, when all the evidence is in, each reader must weight the various testimonies and serve as his own judge and jury. He may consider the evidence damning and once and for all reject the hypothesis of reincarnation. On the other hand, he may consider the evidence inconclusive as yet and decide to further pursue the matter with a mind that is no longer closed to investigations of unorthodox subjects. Whatever his decision, the reader of this book will not run the risk of being found guilty of having judged the mystery without first examining the evidence.

BRAD STEIGER
Decorah, Iowa

REMEMBRANCES OF LIVES PAST

When I began accumulating research materials for this book, I contacted David D. Graham, publisher of *Infinity Newsletter*, and told him of my desire to locate American cases of reincarnation.

Dave commiserated with me by stating that good cases of reincarnation here in the States were difficult to come by. "I assure you that such a book as the one you are working on would be unique, due to the rarity of these cases," he added.

Graham did place my name and address in *Infinity*, however, with a brief note stating the kind of material for which I was searching.

I suppose this chapter could be titled "Bridey Murphy Bible Belt Style," for the individuals who offered their "memories" of a past life were most emphatic that they should do so under the protection and guarantee of complete anonymity.

I did come to one conclusion as the result of my correspondence with those who claim to remember past lives and with those who claim to have hypnotically induced others to recall former incarnations: American cases of reincarnation are not as rare as one at first supposes. What makes these experiences seem so scarce is that it is almost impossible to find individuals to go on record that they have had ostensible memories of previous incarnations.

A Midwestern housewife simply does not broadcast it about that she can regress others to the trance state where they apparently assume past personalities. If she does, she runs the risk of being branded a kook by her neighbors and a heretic by her church.

A bright college student does not recite details of his spontaneous recall of a past life for fear of being identified with the "flower children" who subsist on LSD cubes. If he does insist that his experience was real, he endangers his opportunities for employment upon graduation.

A successful businessman does not drop the bombshell of his recollection of a past life at the executive board meeting, or he will soon be seeking another position.

Such are the difficulties in acquiring substantial cases of reincarnation. "You may use my experience, but under no circumstances are you to identify me!" I have been told on numerous occasions. Most of the alleged cases of reincarnation I would not use under any circumstances—period! Often the alleged former life has clearly been the result of an excessively dramatic dream, an overactive imagination exploiting a psyche prone to suggestion, or, often, a deliberate attempt to "put one over on" the interviewer.

There follow, though, four cases which seem to contain certain convincing elements related by subjects who seem to be of a sincere and trustworthy nature. The names are not the actual names of the people involved.

Case #1: Mrs. Rita Schmidt is an attractive blonde housewife in her mid-twenties. She has two children, is a devout Roman Catholic. Mrs. Schmidt has a most pleasant personality and is well liked by her co-workers on her part-time job.

Last spring Mrs. Schmidt engaged me in conversation concerning certain aspects of psychical research. She said that she had read a number of my books and told me that she had always been interested in the subject.

"What do you think of hypnosis?" she asked after we had visited for a few moments.

Not knowing precisely what information she was seeking by asking such a question, I gave a noncommittal answer. "As I tell my students," I said, "it is nothing to play around with. Serious psychological damage can be done during an amateur experiment in parlor hypnosis—psychological damage that may take years of therapy to correct."

I could tell by the expression on Mrs. Schmidt's face that she had not wanted a lecture on the possible ill effects of amateur experiments in hypnosis. "Do you think it would be possible to bring a person back to another life through hypnosis?" she asked.

I had known Mrs. Schmidt for over two years. If she had not already told me of her interest in ESP research, I would have thought the question most uncharacteristic of her. I live in a small Midwestern village where the most controversial topics discussed by the townspeople have generally to do with how much moisture is good for the corn or who should have been disqualified during last night's stockcar race. I find the solitude and quiet of a small town most conducive to my writing, but I have grown accustomed to the fact that there exist few people in the village with whom I might discuss my research. It turned out that I had unjustly placed Mrs. Schmidt in the category of the Not Interested.

"Some researchers believe that one might be able to recall a past life while in a deep hypnotic trance," I said cautiously, wanting Mrs. Schmidt to declare herself further.

The attractive young blonde matron was not one to hesitate. "Well, I've done it," she announced with a slight blush. "I brought my sister back to another incarnation."

When Mrs. Schmidt was 15, she had bought a paper-back book on hypnosis. A natural hypnotist, she was soon able to place subjects into the trance state after a quick reading of the book.

Although one of her sisters resisted Mrs. Schmidt's hypnotic powers, her younger sister proved to be an excellent subject. "She knew I wouldn't hurt her and she trusted me completely," Mrs. Schmidt said.

Soon word got around the small high school about the teen-aged hypnotist in their midst. Recess periods became much livelier now that Rita had acquired her hypnotic prowess.

One day, during history class, the instructor began to scoff at his student's claims and challenged her to demonstrate her ability right there in the classroom.

Such a skeptic-packed audience would have made a professional hypnotist nervous. The conditions were not at all conducive toward an effective display of hypnosis. The room was brightly lighted, her classmates were tittering, and her history instructor was glaring his cynicism.

Rita selected the biggest boy in the room as her subject. In spite of the unsatisfactory conditions under which she was forced to perform, she soon had her subject entranced.

"I'll prove it," she announced to her surprised instructor. "I'll prove he's really under."

Rita took a straight pin and jabbed it into the boy's upraised palm. There was no tell-tale flinch of pain to testify that he was still awake and serving as a co-conspirator in any scheme of Rita's.

By the time Rita had finished putting her classmate through his paces, the history instructor was no longer skeptical of his student's prowess as a first-class amateur hypnotist.

Rita was ready to advance to new hypnotic horizons

by the time that summer vacation had come. Her paperback book was dog-eared and worn; its pages loose and wrinkled. She had virtually memorized all of its contents.

"Betty," she said one day as she and her sister lay on the lawn in the shade of a large tree. "How would you like to try an experiment?"

"Sure," her sister agreed. "Like what?"

"Like having me hypnotize you and see if you can remember any past lives."

"Do you think we should?" Betty wondered. "I mean, is that sort of thing right?"

"You trust me, don't you? I won't let anything happen to you."

Soon Betty was lying relaxed, as her older sister spoke to her in soothing tones.

"You are now growing younger," Rita told her. "You will remember only pleasant experiences in your past. You are growing younger, younger, younger. You are moving back through time, younger, younger, younger. You are going back through time and space, growing younger, still younger. Now you are nine, eight, seven, six . . . younger, younger, five . . . four . . . three . . . two . . . one. . . .

"Now you are going farther back. Back to before you were born. You are going back into a life which you lived before. I will count from six to zero and when I reach zero, I will count from zero to eighteen. When I reach eighteen, you will be able to look around you and tell me all about yourself and what you see in your previous life. You will be able to speak to me in English."

Rita began counting, first from six to zero, then from zero to eighteen.

"You are now eighteen years old," she told her sister when she had counted off the last digit. "You are living in a life before this one. You can look around and tell me what you see. You will tell me about yourself in English."

Betty opened her eyes, looked about, began to talk excitedly in a foreign tongue.

Rita's mouth dropped open in amazement. "English," she managed at last. "You will speak to me in English!"

She repeated the command three times before the voice heeded her word.

"What is your name?" Rita asked.

Betty replied with a name that sounded like "Alana." This could possibly have been Elena or Elaine.

"Where do you live?"

Again the answer was unclear, but the word sounded like "Sana."

"How are you dressed?"

"In a lovely long dress of many colors." (Betty was wearing shorts.)

"What color is your hair?"

"It is very black and I wear it long." (Betty and Rita are both blondes.)

"What color are your eyes?"

"Blue." (Betty also has blue eyes.)

Rita continued to question the personality, Alana, fascinatedly taking down notes on their strange conversation. Then, all at once, she began to experience a sensation of dread and unease. She decided to bring Betty "back" to the present.

"I am now going to bring you back," Rita said, trying desperately to keep her voice calm. She gave the exact day of the week and the month, and the year—even the correct time.

"I will count from eighteen to zero, then from one to thirteen. When I finish counting, you will be here in the present, thirteen years old."

Rita was most relieved when Betty returned as Betty and not as "Alana." She tried the experiment one more time, and Betty once again relived a brief period of time as "Alana." Then doctor, clergyman, and parent learned of the teenager's experiments and sternly called a halt to her using her younger sister as a "guinea pig."

"Someday," Mrs. Schmidt said, "my sister and I might try the experiments again. I believe that my sister really did begin to relive a past life."

Case #2: Mark Whitman is a bright college student from Chicago. A bespectacled business major, Mark is typical of today's hard-working, no-nonsense college men. The world of the contemporary Joe College may be a sphere of beautiful foldout girls, all night bull sessions concerning various "playboy" philosophies, and a yearning for the "good life," but the environment of the male student is also one of great tensions and frustrations and the ominous knowledge that to goof-off is to invite academic failure and thereby hasten a stint in the armed forces.

Today's college student has been conditioned to sharply differentiate between what is real and what is unreal, between what constitutes reality and what constitutes fantasy. Most college students have long since traded in their desire to seek a "somewhere over the rainbow" for a social security card. Materialism is the philosophy which shapes their appraisal of "borderline" experience, and if they cannot touch, see, smell, or hear it, they will not believe it. Speculation is reserved only for what has already been accepted by the scientific Establishment.

Mark was a typical child of his time until he went abroad on a six-week summer study program. The result of the trip was to be a paper comparing the various economic systems of Europe with that of the United States. The son of a well-to-do businessman, Mark's basic passion was the world of high finance. He seldom discussed other subjects, and he had a limited range of interests beyond the future of the marketplace. In fact, it took a concentrated effort on the part of Mark's friends and the accompanying faculty advisor to talk the young man into a day of sight-seeing in the historic German city where they were awaiting the arrival of another group of students from the States.

Mark made little effort to hide his boredom as the guide led the small group of tourists through one of the massive castles which had been reconditioned for sight-seeing. Then, in spite of himself, Mark began to take a keen interest in the German guide's recitation of the events of historical significance which had taken place in or near the castle.

He felt his breathing become deeper and quicken. There was something about the stone hallways, the armor on the walls, the paintings, the feel of the rough floor beneath his feet that began to seem strangely familiar.

". . . and this passageway leads to a dead-end," the guide was saying. "The hall ends at a wall of solid stone."

"Not so," Mark blurted out. And no one appeared more startled at his comment than he. The guide stared at him as if one of the suits of armor had suddenly spoken. Seldom did anyone interrupt his tour lecture, and no one had ever stopped his recitation to argue. These rude Americans!

"What did you say, Mark?" the faculty advisor to the group of young economists asked.

"I—I said that the guide is wrong when he says that passageway leads to a dead-end," Mark replied.

The German guide regarded the young American coolly. "So how is it that I am wrong?" he demanded of his questioner.

"Tell him, Mark," one of his friends laughed. "Ol' Mark, who nearly flunked European history, is now going to lecture on Rhine castles!"

Mark was blushing furiously. "What I say is true."

"Well, then," the guide snapped, unholstering a flashlight, "let us walk down the passageway and see who is correct!"

"Mark," the faculty adviser sighed, glancing at his watch, "time is growing short and we have other places to see. Why don't you just apologize to the guide and let us continue?"

"No!" the guide said firmly. "This young man called me a liar, and I must prove to him that he is wrong!"

"I didn't call you a liar," Mark objected. "I only meant that you were mistaken in saying that the passageway leads to a wall of stone."

The guide turned on his heel. "Follow me then!"

After the guide had led the members of the group who had elected to follow him about sixty feet down the dark passageway, he played his flashlight beam triumphantly over a dank wall.

"Do you not call that a wall?" he asked Mark. "Is that not a wall of solid stone?"

Mark leaned his hand against the damp surface of the stone. "No," he said, slowly shaking his head. "There is a room beyond. A small room, but it is a room, nonetheless. This wall has been added at a relatively recent period of time."

A collective groan went up from Mark's fellow students. "Cool it, Mark," one advised him. "Leave it alone so we can get on with the tour."

"But he seems so certain," said a well-dressed Englishwoman, who had followed the group down the dank passageway out of curiosity. "Isn't there someway you might check it for him?"

The guide looked as if he were considering providing the tourists with yet another rare sight, that of spontaneous human combustion.

Deciding upon self-control as the best means of keeping his job, the guide showed his teeth in an official smile. "Today is Wednesday. The curator is in his office on the main floor today. Perhaps if the young man will speak to the curator he will be satisfied. Now, let the rest of us continue our tour!"

To the amazement of his classmates, Mark did not let the matter drop. Two of them, together with their faculty adviser, left the main group of tourists and followed their determined friend to the curator's office.

The curator listened patiently to Mark's story, asking him occasionally to repeat certain phrases, because, as he explained, his "American was not as okay as it should be."

"You are quite mistaken, young friend," the historian said with a note of finality after Mark had completed his contention that a room existed beyond the stone wall which sealed off the ancient corridor.

"Can't you check it?" Mark asked. "I'm certain that you are wrong."

The curator arched a craggy eyebrow, then scowled. "What is it that makes you such an authority on this castle?" he wanted to know.

But by now Mark's fierce determination had become contagious. "You must have some old blueprints of the castle," the faculty adviser said. "Perhaps you can match them against Mark's story."

The curator broke his stony silence by suddenly reaching for a cardboard tube on a filing cabinet behind him. With the tip of his pipe he began pushing a rolled up map through the cylinder. "Here is a blueprint made of the castle in 1896. . . ."

"Oh, much too late," Mark said, shaking his head. "This castle was built in the 12th century."

"There simply aren't many blueprints lying about from the 12th century," the curator said, resuming his scowl.

Mark reached for pen and paper, sketched a diagram of the room which he insisted lay beyond the stone wall. After he had finished his drawing, he named a German book. He smacked his lips after speaking the title, as if the Germanic words tasted strangely on his tongue. Mark's friends knew that he spoke only an elementary German.

For the first time the curator seemed to hear the young American. His scowl deepened, and his jaws clamped tightly on his pipe stem. He repeated the name of the volume, then directed a question to Mark in German.

When Mark only stared back at him incomprehendingly, the scholar shrugged and turned to his bookshelves.

A few moments later, the curator was blowing dust off an ancient volume. Carefully he turned the crisp and yellowed pages. Then, with a grunt of surprise, he set the book before the waiting Americans.

"It is as our young friend says," the curator admitted, indicating a diagram on a page of the open book. "Originally the passageway extended to this small room. See, his drawing matches exactly with the plan in this book."

"But how did you know, Mark?" the faculty adviser asked his student.

Mark Whitman has been trying to answer that question ever since.

Did he pick up a memory pattern that had somehow charged the stones of the old castle?

Had he clairvoyantly divined the location of the secret room? Or had he come across another copy of the ancient book at some earlier time, forgotten the incident, and stored away the knowledge of the hidden room in his subconscious?

If one does not accept any of these hypotheses, then one is confronted with the alternative which Mark Whitman does not enjoy considering. One must believe that, in some earlier existence, Mark Whitman walked the passageways of that ancient castle, unhindered by the stone wall. Perhaps the room which the thick wall had hidden might even have been his own.

Case #3: From her earliest childhood, Ethel Hanson had had a repetitive dream experience.

In this strange dream, Ethel saw herself laughing in a raucous manner and swinging her body about in an abandoned and frenzied dance. She saw herself surrounded by the leaping flames of campfires. She heard the mounting tempo of clapping hands, the wild and sensuous music rising to a climax of violent abandon. And always she was dancing, dancing like some unrestrained creature of pagan pleasures.

The most paradoxical aspect of Ethel's dream was that she was the daughter of a strict Methodist minister, who considered any aspect of the dance as Satan's own jig.

When she was a child of eight, Ethel's father caught her dancing in front of the radio (a radio was permitted because of the news programs). She was spanked with the full force of her father's righteous indignation and forbidden to ever listen to those "infernal disc jockeys" again.

At age eleven, Ethel had not yet learned to leave well enough alone. She came home from school one afternoon and asked her mother if she might take dancing lessons with two of her girlfriends. Her horrified mother duly reported the request to Ethel's father, who not only took her allowance away for two weeks but forbade her to continue her friendship with the two "dancing daughters of the devil."

By the time she was a teenager, Ethel had learned that dancing was only engaged in by young ladies who did not value their reputations, and while her friends were having supervised record parties in the homes of "hedonistic parents," Ethel was sitting at home with a book from her father's "approved" reading list.

And yet in her dreams she would dance, dance, dance. And how glorious it was! Her hair was borne on the night wind like the mane of some marvelously spirited mare. She knew she was barefooted. She could feel her bare feet striking the smooth earth with a rhythm that made her blood course hotly through her veins. And she would swirl her skirt—swirl and twist it high so that her flashing ankles and full thighs inflamed the senses of the cheering men.

Mornings, she would awaken feeling unclean and wonder why God had sent such obscene visions to torment her. She considered confiding in her mother, but she knew that the story of the secret dream would soon find its way to her father's ears. She took no pleasure in the prospect that Reverend Hanson might try to beat the Devil out of her.

"Life," Ethel Hanson wrote, "had settled into a rut of incredible frustration and torment. When I entered college and began to take some psychology courses, I theorized that my dream was a wish fulfillment. That is, I was dreaming about dancing because I was not permitted by my parents to go to dances. I further observed that most girls my age did like to dance, and it was natural that I should have been so much in love with dancing even as a little girl."

Ethel had found the solution to the repetitive dream. Or so she believed.

It was at a New Year's Eve party that Ethel Hanson became more confused than she had ever been concerning the source of the strange and sensual night scene which she had witnesses since her childhood.

Ethel was a senior at the small church college which she attended, and would be graduating that June as a social worker. Although she was regarded by all who knew her as an exceedingly prim and proper young woman, she was lovely and gracious enough never to lack boyfriends. Many were attracted but few were chosen, of course, because Reverend Hanson conducted an extensive screening of the young men who came to pay court to any one of his five daughters.

On this particular New Year's Eve, the clergyman had been more intent on preparing the New Year's Day sermon than in examining the moral credentials of the young man who had asked Ethel to accompany him to a "quiet, well-chaperoned party."

Charlie Norris, who had graduated from high school with Ethel, was known to have stretched the truth on more than one occasion, to have swallowed the contents of several bottles of beer and, when he could get it, hard liquor, and he had boasted to any of his contemporaries who would listen that he intended to "thaw out that preacher's daughter."

The party, in short, was not the quiet, sober, little get-together that Charlie had talked of to Reverend Hanson. It was a noisy, liquor-sopping, jam-packed blast!

Ethel had a few moments of inner panic, but she got a good grip on Charlie's arm and entered the party fully determined to enjoy herself. She was, after all, going on 22.

Ethel did, however, make Charlie promise "not to try to get her to take a drink." This was one promise that Charlie kept. He did not have to tease, cajole, or shame her into drinking. The innocent appearing fruit punch was laced with enough vodka to quench the thirst of the entire Bolshoi Ballet.

By the time the party-goers had assembled to play "Amateur Hour," Ethel was feeling so uninhibited that she had actually laughed at one of Charlie's off-color stories.

"Amateur Hour," Charlie explained to the group, was

an old and honored tradition among the young people who had been gathering for New Year's Eve since the parent-chaperoned pop and popcorn parties of junior high school days. According to the rules, each guest at the party must perform for the group when called upon or be subject to the committees' choosing a prank for him to suffer through.

The first guest called upon a young woman, sang "God Bless America" in a high, cracking soprano. The second contestant earned a solid round of applause for his imitation of their old high school principal.

Ethel was relieved to note that the critical standards of the audience had been suitably blunted by large doses of liquor. Although she felt a slight repugnance at the sight of all her old high school friends in varying stages of inebriation, she was grateful that they would not be in any condition to place high demands upon the performances of the contestants in the amateur hour. She was grateful, too, that she had her wits about her and was in complete control of the situation. She called for Charlie to bring her another cup of that delicious fruit punch.

By the time Ethel Hanson was called to the floor by the master of ceremonies, there was a wicked sparkle in her eyes. Ethel was known to have a fine choir voice, so a reasonably sober young man had already taken his place at the piano in anticipation of her wishing to sing for her entertainment.

Ethel Hanson shocked all assembled by announcing that she intended to dance. Most of the young people in the room had known Ethel since grade school. They knew full well the position of her clergyman father on the evils of dancing. If they were shocked at Ethel's announcement, they were open-mouthed and wide-eyed when, after she requested that her accompanist play some "wild gypsy music," she put on a demonstration of

31

the most abandoned and exotic dancing that any of them had ever witnessed.

Her hair, worn sedately in a bun piled atop her head, was undone and allowed to flow in sleek, dark ripples down to her shoulders. Her shoes were kicked into a corner and, barefooted, she executed difficult dance steps with style and grace. She tipped back her head and laughed at the almost hypnotic effect her swirling skirt was having on the men in the crowd.

On and on she danced until she collapsed into the arms of a very pale Charlie Norris.

When Ethel Hanson regained her sense of the present, she refused to believe the reports her friends made of her performance. She remembered nothing after she moved through the crowd to the piano. She recalled that she had intended to ask the accompanist if he knew the melody of a popular ballad so that she might sing, but beyond that moment, she could recollect nothing.

"But you danced like a professional," one of her girl friends told her.

"Like a gypsy!" put in another.

As her friends described her dance, Ethel felt a strange little hollow being clawed away in the pit of her stomach. They were describing her dream! They had seen her as she had been seeing herself in the secret dream that had been haunting her since childhood.

Since that night, Ethel has often tried to recapture the grace and skill which she displayed at the party. Her efforts, as described by her close friends, have been "clumsy and awkward." Charlie Norris confessed to her about the vodka in the punch, but Ethel Hanson has refused to become intoxicated in an attempt to recreate the wild experience of her dream.

She did receive an interesting letter from a girl friend who attends another college. The friend, a very talented and agile dancer, attempted to reproduce the dance steps, which she had seen Ethel execute, for one of her instructors, a Spaniard with a great interest in his country's folk music.

"He said that I was dancing a very old dance of the *gitana*, the gypsies of Spain," she wrote Ethel, "and he asked me wherever had I seen such a dance performed."

Has Ethel's recurrent dream been a vivid memory of a previous life? Or do her psychology texts contain the correct answers when they speak of repression and wish fulfillment? We will never know unless Ethel Hanson chooses once more to imbibe of spiked punch or consents to undergo hypnotic regression.

Case #4: "I shouldn't even be telling you this," John Stevenson wrote. "I have a good business in a small town, and I am the scoutmaster for our local troop. If word got out that I believed or thought I believed in such a thing as reincarnation, I would suddenly become a kook, my business would die, and people would start spreading rumors that I was a pervert, so I couldn't work with the boy scouts any more!"

John Stevenson's glimpse at the unknown came while he was on a camping trip with nine boy scouts. Their plan was to hike up to Indian Cave, camp there overnight, then return before dusk on the following day.

"Indian Cave is a local landmark," Stevenson explained. "It is in a beautiful location down by the river, so it makes an ideal spot at which to camp. Not too many people like to trek to the cave, because there are no roads leading to it, so that makes it remote enough to give the boys an illusion of really roughing it.

"The walls of the cave still bear the evidence of ancient campfires. The arrowheads and Indian artifacts have long since been picked up, but there are still some old cave paintings which the Indians made. Some people say the paintings are fake and that the Indians didn't really make them, but they look pretty genuine to me."

Stevenson led his group of boy scouts to the cave that day and set them to work building campfires and clearing ground for their sleeping bags and tents. Later, enough of them caught trout in a nearby stream to supplement the provisions which they had brought from home.

After the usual campfire songs and hair-raising assortment of "real" ghost stories, Stevenson told his young charges to turn in. He sat up for a while, smoking his pipe before the fire, until each of the boys had begun the regular breathing that told him they were all asleep.

Stevenson crawled into his own sleeping bag. He remembers thinking about what a beautiful night it was when ". . . the weird part of all this comes.

"I suppose I could have been dreaming, but it all seems too real to have been a dream. I don't know if it was the power of suggestion, sleeping there next to that old cave or what, but I all of a sudden had this feeling that I had slept on that same ground a long time ago. Only then I had been an Indian.

"I remember sitting up and feeling strange. Like you sometimes feel when you wake up in a strange hotel room and you don't know where you are for a few minutes. I looked at my hands and bare arms and seemed satisfied that they were now brown-skinned instead of white. I got up and looked at my reflection in the moonlight on the water. I couldn't see all of my face, because it was too dark, but I could see enough to know that it was a different face from the one I have now, yet I knew that *it* was my face, too. I could see that I had long, shoulder-length hair, and it looked like I had some kind of beadwork pattern across the chest of my shirt.

"I just had this kind of wonderful feeling that I had come back to a very familiar place where I had had a lot

of happy memories . . . as an Indian. The whole dream
or vision or whatever it was was filled with my doing
just simple little things. I mean, it wasn't a big Sitting
Bull versus General Custer type thing, and I guess that
was what made it all seem so real.

"I especially remember walking into the cave and
looking at the drawings on the wall. I seemed to hold a
burning branch in my hand for light. I smiled and
nodded my head. For the first time the drawings seemed
to make sense to me. In fact, as I walked under the
stars, the whole world seemed to make sense to me. Like
there really was a Divine Plan and a logic to the universe.

"I don't know. Say it was just a dream if you want to,
but it seemed so real to me that I just have to believe
that I've been walking around on this earth in one form
or another for a long, long time."

John Stevenson, as we shall see, is not alone in this
strange conviction that he has lived before and has
been able to recall memories of past incarnations.

"THEM DAMN YANKEES SHOT ME"

One of the most thoroughly documented and well-
researched cases suggestive of reincarnation in recent
years was published recently in the December 1966
issue of *Fate*. The article, "Reincarnation of a Civil
War Victim," described the hypnotically induced regression of a New Hampshire high school boy to his life as
a farmer in Jefferson, North Carolina, during the period
of 1840 to 1863.

The author of the piece, Loring G. Williams, was a high school teacher who had developed a reputation for hypnotic prowess. "Bill" has often been called upon to provide entertainment for local fund-raising drives; and as a member of the Keene State College Psychic Research Society, he has participated in several investigations into the nature of psychic phenomena.

I contacted "Bill" Williams and told him of my proposed book on reincarnation.

"I'll help you all I can," Williams said, generously. "Some new material has developed since the *Fate* article appeared. For one thing, the boy has recalled additional lives."

Williams told me that it would take him quite a while to make transcripts of all the tape recordings, but he promised to provide me with material just as soon as he could.

In much less time than I expected, a large packet of materials arrived from Williams. He had worked overtime to get the information to me as quickly as possible. Briefly, here is the story of "Jonathan" as it was reported in *Fate*.

George Field, a 15-year-old neighbor of Williams, decided one evening to sit in on the weekly sessions which the teacher-hypnotist had been holding in his home. During these meetings, Williams would regress volunteers in the hope that he might find a subject whose story could be checked.

Such a search is not an easy one. As Williams put it, many subjects, when regressed, are hazy about details. They cannot remember their full names or their parents' names, are not sure where they lived, and are unable to give other details that would be needed to check a story. Others, though they may go into vivid detail, describe an existence so long ago, or in so remote a place, that checking is out of the question. Then along came George.

George Field proved to be an ideal subject for hypnosis. He went easily into trance and was amenable to hypnotic suggestion. Within a short time, George was describing a past existence which had taken place in North Carolina at a point in history which would be near enough to check out.

While in deep hypnotic trance, the New Hampshire teenager "remembered" a life as "Jonathan Powell." He recalled that his father's name had been Willard and that his paternal grandmother was named Mary. He could not remember the name of his mother.

According to "Jonathan," his father worked a small farm and labored in the nearby tin mine. The family were Quakers, ministered to by a traveling parson named Brown. Mr. Brown lived in the "villie" of Jefferson in Ashe County.

Williams continued to move George-Jonathan forward and backward in the time sequence of his lifetime. As the boy spoke, a tape-recorder caught every word so that, if possible, Williams could substantiate the physical existence of Jonathan Powell.

Finally, the hypnotist took Jonathan up his last day in that incarnation. When Williams asked the personality what he was doing, Jonathan replied that he was busy loading potatoes for those "damn Yankee soldiers."

According to Jonathan, the soldiers were willing to pay only a few cents a bushel for the crop which he had worked so hard to harvest. He cursed the men in their gray uniforms.

Williams queried Jonathan on this point. If the soldiers were wearing gray, they must have been southerners, not yankees.

"They ain't southerners," Jonathan said firmly. But the farmer was more concerned about the men who were surrounding him than their color uniforms. They wanted five sacks of potatoes, but they weren't getting them for ten cents a bushel! The stubborn farmer told the soldiers to keep their money.

Then George-Jonathan made terrible sounds of pain and began to cough.

William spoke softly to him, tried to reassure him that all was well, and let him speak again.

When the hypnotist had taken away the awful hurt, Jonathan told him that he had been shot in the stomach by the plundering soldiers because he would not take their "damn money." The personality complained that it still "hurt a little."

Williams progressed the farmer another five minutes in the time of his last day of that incarnation. When he asked the personality what he felt at that point, Jonathan answered that he could feel nothing.

At the count of three, Williams brought the boy back to the present.

Williams was most eager to travel to Jefferson, North Carolina, to substantiate Jonathan's story and to attempt to confirm the physical existence of the personality from whom he had learned the apparent details of a previous earth life.

Due to the limitations of a close budget, Williams, his son Jack, and George Field, decided to make a camping trip to Jefferson just as soon as school was out for the summer.

"Camping was a new experience for me," Williams wrote to me, "although both boys had had considerable experience with camporees in the Boy Scouts and had quite a bit of equipment. George had a tent that would sleep three, and between us we had plenty of sleeping bags. A friend provided camping stoves. Finally, much to my wife's dismay, a pile of equipment began to form on the dining room table, ready to be packed. Since we were traveling by Volkswagen, a careful list had to be made and every unnecessary item eliminated. We did consider it very necessary that we take my two tape recorders—the large one on which to play the tapes made in Keene (at the home of the president of the New Hampshire Psychic Research Society) and, if needed, to tape any conversations which we might have there where A.C. power was available, and a small portable for use in the car in and around Jefferson."

Williams was fortunate in that he had an old army buddy, who was now a minister serving a congregation in Watuga, Tennessee, living in Johnson City, just a short distance from Jefferson, North Carolina. The clergyman's backyard provided the expedition from New Hampshire with a base of operations from which to conduct its research in Jefferson.

Williams' enthusiasm and his hopes were high. He had visions of Jonathan-George running about recognizing familiar landmarks, leading them to his mother's grave, falling weeping upon his own burial place. Then it would be a simple matter to proceed to the courthouse and find all the records which would substantiate the previous existence of George Field in the physical person of Jonathan Powell.

"Things did not work out that way," Williams says.

Upon approaching the village, George claims to have had strong feelings that he had been there before. Williams placed the teenager into a deep trance and regressed him to 1860. As he brought the boy's personality back to become Jonathan once again, he cautioned the lad to pay no attention to automobiles or other modern contrivances. Williams wished to take no chances on frightening Jonathan or to distract him with the puzzling artifacts of the twentieth century.

When Jonathan opened his eyes to Jefferson for the

first time in over a hundred years, he was completely dismayed.

"Picture yourself, if you can," William writes, "going back to your old neighborhood after a hundred years. There are all new houses and streets, and you are trying to find your own back yard."

When the investigators visited the Ashe County courthouse in Jefferson, they were disappointed to learn that the county had not recorded births and deaths before 1921! There had, however, been a registry of deeds.

On Page 430, Volume A, Williams and the boys found the copy of a deed in which a Stephen Reed had conveyed to a Mary Powell a parcel of land in 1803. This discovery excited the group very much. Jonathan had named a Mary Powell as his paternal grandmother. In 1803, Mary Powell would have been about the right age to be buying farm land. The investigators became even more sure of their research when they were told that Powell was a very uncommon name in that area.

The register of deeds referred Williams to a local historian who might be able to tell them the genealogy of the old families of Ashe County. Williams called the historian and made an appointment with her for that afternoon.

When the historian learned the purpose of Williams' expedition into North Carolina, she went firmly on record as saying that she did not believe in "this sort of thing."

She did, however, agree to offer what help she could. And, after listening to the tape recording of George-Jonathan's session at the Keene Psychical Research Society, she had to confess that she was most impressed with "Jonathan's" knowledge of Ashe County.

After the historian had heard the tape, Williams regressed George to Jonathan so that the woman might question the personality concerning the Ashe County of 1860.

"Remember to keep your questions in the present tense," Williams cautioned the historian. "To Jonathan it still *is* 1860!"

The historian queried Jonathan about a total of 25 persons and events in the history of Jefferson. Writing in *Fate* Williams said that Jonathan knew nothing about some of them. He did, however, claim to know about 15 of them, many in detail. He mentioned such things as these people's financial status, their children's names, and when they built their houses. These details proved to be substantially correct. In the author's opinion he gave enough detailed answers to make any possibility of chance very remote.

In addition to the historian's confirming Jonathan's knowledge of the people and events of Jefferson circa 1860, she substantiated his claim that there had been a Mr. Brown who had served as a circuit riding preacher. She could find no records of a Quaker church, but she rapidly conceded that a group might have met in private homes.

They replayed the tape which they had made when the historian questioned Jonathan about his life in Jefferson, Williams wrote. They wanted to once again get her reaction to his answers. To Williams, it seemed amazing and very significant that one who had never had any connection with Jefferson could know so much about it.

Williams recalls a humorous incident which occurred while he was riding about Jefferson with George and Jack. The boys asked him what the "snuff" was that they had seen for sale in numerous places in the village. In New Hampshire and in New England in general, the taking of snuff is practically a lost "art." Later that day, while shopping at a supermarket, Williams bought a can of snuff as a souvenir for each of the boys.

Williams had worked in the South and had seen the chewing tobacco used on many occasions. He explained to the boys what little he knew about the "taking" of snuff.

"About all I could really remember," Williams says, "is that the old-timers used to pack a wad behind the lip to get the flavor from it."

As the three of them were riding around the countryside a bit later, Williams regressed George to Jonathan. He hoped that Jonathan might recognize some landmarks and locate his farm, but then, suddenly, another idea occurred to the hypnotist.

"How do you like snuff, Jonathan?" he asked. "Do you want some?"

"I shore do!"

Jonathan had trouble getting the snuff out of "that kind of a box," but once he had the tobacco tin open, he set about "blowing" it in a skilled and expert manner.

Williams was startled. He had never seen anyone "sniff" the tobacco up the nose before. It took him a few puzzled moments before he remembered an article he had read which described this manner of using snuff as being the most popular method years ago. But it was still amazing to watch someone actually "sniffing" tobacco. It was an accomplishment which obviously took considerable practice and experience, not to mention a strong nose! Williams knew that George had never seen this done.

In his evaluation of the tape as compared with the uncovered evidence, Williams points out the difficulty of substantiating such a nondescript life as Jonathan Powell's one hundred years after his death. At the same time, the hypnotist stresses the fact that Jonathan-George spoke of an obscure village in a small North Carolina county, a place of which George Field would hardly be aware. "Jonathan" was able to identify and provide details of the lives of several old families of Ashe County. He was able to identify much of the county's topography, which no maps of the area name. Then, too, there was a Mary Powell—a woman with an uncommon surname for the county—who bought farm land and who would have been the right age to be Jonathan's grandmother, just as the personality claimed.

Williams feels that one of the most significant parts of the tape is Jonathan's description of his death. Jonathan claimed that he was shot to death by Yankee soldiers in *gray* uniforms, because he refused to sell them potatoes. Even the most casual student of American history knows that the Yankees wore *blue* uniforms. Furthermore, Williams' research established the fact that there were no Northern troops in North Carolina in 1863.

"Once again, though," Williams says, "Jonathan was right. The local historian told me that at that time, there were bands of renegades who came down from the north, using the war as an excuse to raid and plunder. They could well have been dressed in gray because they would have stolen their uniforms."

Shortly after the article appeared in *Fate*, Williams and George Field received further substantiation of Jonathan's existence in a letter from a woman who claimed to be the great-niece of Jonathan Powell. The woman went on to clear up a number of items which were unclearly stated by the personality of Jonathan.

"He (Jonathan), was killed by the Yankees, so my father said; but he didn't know any details at all about the case on how he was killed. Willard Powell was Jonathan's brother. Jim Powell was Jonathan's father [Jonathan stated that his father's name was Willard and that he could not remember having a brother]—and he was red-headed, or sandy haired; and all the family had blue eyes. We never knew what became of Willard or his family.

". . . My mother often talked about the Quakers and they would spend the night with her family over there. There was no Quaker church. . . .

". . . I haven't done any research on history, but a lot of those eastern Tennessee men fought for the South. That could have been some of them in the gray uniforms that killed Jonathan or it could have been the renegades."

In subsequent sessions of hypnotic regression, Williams has led George Field back into three lives prior to his incarnation as Jonathan Powell.

"These were short lives in England in the fifteen and sixteen hundreds, so they are impossible to check," Williams told me. "They do, however, paint a vivid and seemingly accurate picture of life during those periods. In two cases, he was a girl, once a boy. In no case did he or she know his parents. It is a historic fact that during those years there were thousands of orphaned or deserted children living in the streets."

Although the transcripts of each of the lives is quite lengthy, Williams provided me with a capsule report of the three previous incarnations of George Field before he was born as Jonathan.

Number One. A girl. She has no memory of parents. She first remembers being cared for by a man who seems to be no relation. She lives in a one-room hovel and sleeps on a board. She is alone most of the time, and the man brings her just enough food to keep her alive. When she is about seven years old, the man dies. She takes to the streets, sleeping where she can, eating raw dough stolen from bakeries and whatever else can be found. When she is about 12 years old she is killed in the street by a horse and wagon. (A note of great interest here!

This is the manner in which Jonathan said that his mother died. Could this mean something?)

Number Two. A girl. Her background and living conditions are similar to Number One. The most interesting thing about this experiment is that when taken through the death experience, she accounted all the symptoms of the Black Plague that swept England at the time.

Number Three. A boy. In this incarnation, he is again orphaned and deserted. [Jonathan could not remember his father, only that he had died at an early age. George Field lives with his widowed mother. Again, could a pattern be maintained in reincarnation?] As a twelve-or fourteen-year old boy, he works around the docks and is on the sailing ships in port there. He seldom receives any pay, but he is given food for working. He enjoys most the work on the sails and the rigging.

The most amazing thing about this account, Williams relates, is that when he regressed George Field to this life, he asked the sixteenth century teenager if he could splice rope.

"I splice a lot of it," the personality told him.

Williams produced a piece on which the boy made a fast and expert splice. George Field has not even the faintest idea of how to go about splicing a rope. Rope splicing has become almost a lost art since the days of sailing vessels.

In life Number Three, George fell off the dock and drowned when he was about fifteen.

Loring G. Williams has numerous other cases in his files. At my request, he capsulized five major subjects whose claims of past lives are currently being investigated.

Subject Number One. In this present incarnation, Subject Number One is a woman of 25. While under hypnosis, Williams has allowed her to recall two other lives.

Her first remembered incarnation took place in the United States about 1850, when she was born a boy who lived with his mother and sister in a cabin on a small farm. There was no father present, and the boy seems to feel that his sire has deserted them. When he is about ten years old, he leaves the cabin to go in search of his father. He realizes that the search is hopeless, but he does not return home. Instead, he becomes a drummer boy for the Union during the Civil War. After the War, he becomes a hermit-like creature who prefers to live alone in the woods for the rest of his long life. He acquires many animal friends in this strange, idyllic existence, but he becomes a misanthrope before he dies of old age.

In the woman's second remembered life, she is born a girl in England in 1678. Her parents die when she is about twelve, leaving only a small inheritance on which she might subsist. For two years she manages, then, at fourteen, she has spent all of her money. She is caught stealing and sent to jail. She spends a long time in jail and contracts tuberculosis before she is finally released on the condition that she sign a bond or indentured paper. The papers are sold to a ship captain who transports her to America for the purpose of selling the bond to someone in need of a servant (this was an old racket in those days).

By the time she has reached the colonies, she is weak, coughing a lot, and spitting up blood. She is sold to a plantation near Richmond where she works in the kitchen. She is the only white help there and she describes making many loaves of bread each day. She portrays the large brick oven in detail.

She enjoys life on the plantation much better than England, but her tuberculosis grows progressively worse.

She dies at seventeen. She describes her funeral and watches herself being buried. She is glad that she died because she loves to float.

Subject Number Two. This volunteer for Williams' experiments is a boy who is presently sixteen years old. He has recalled two previous lives under hypnosis.

In his first life, he was born in Illinois about 1830-40. He has a small farm, a wife, and children. When the Civil War starts, he goes to Virginia and joins the Confederate Army. He experiences combat and is killed in action May 5, 1863, probably at the battle of Chancellorville. Williams has spent some time checking the records at Chancellorville, but of approximately 20,000 Confederate soldiers killed there, only a few hundred were ever identified.

The second life which Subject Number Two recalls carries him much farther back into time than the Battle of Chancellorville. He remembers being a black male slave, who was born in ancient Egypt. He is forced to labor a fourteen-hour day with two meals per day as the architects of the Pharoah construct a pyramid. Depressed at last with his hopeless life, he attacks a guard and is put to death at about the age of forty.

Subject Number Three. This 35-year-old woman recalls one previous life. While under hypnotic control, she has regressed to the memory patterns of her life as a girl born in this country to parents of French extraction in the year 1790.

As a young girl, she is sent to France to become a governess for a rich family there. While working in this capacity, she meets a rich, old Frenchman and proceeds to marry him, strictly for his money. After she has the man committed to the satisfying of her desires, she enjoys making his life, and the lives of his servants, just as miserable as she can.

The old man finally dies, much to her delight, leaving her the house, money, jewels, and servants. She becomes involved with a handsome young fortune hunter, who manages to relieve her of most of her money, but she still has her jewels. At last a maid, who has grown weary of her cruelty, kills her and steals her jewels.

Subject Number Four. This sixteen-year-old boy is able to remember owning a plantation and many slaves in the Kentucky of 1840. He recalls his wife and family. Most of all, he remembers the terrible Panic of 1857 when he is unable to sell his sorghum crop. By 1858, he has no money to feed his slaves. They revolt and kill him. After his death, he is able to watch over his family for about ten years, especially one son, who fought throughout the Civil War.

Subject Number Five. Williams' hypnotic prowess has enabled this woman, who is now 28, to relive a past life as the daughter of a noble family in Poland in the early 1800's. True to the custom of the day, the subject remembers that her marriage was arranged for her by her family. She is pleased to discover that her young nobleman is handsome. In addition, he has a great estate, many serfs, and is governor of a territory. When she is about 40, she is thrown from her horse and killed. She has a huge funeral, which she is able to watch. She is also able to watch her family for several years after her death.

"Unfortunately the written word cannot convey the feeling that is expressed in the voice and actions of the subjects as they recount their past lives," Williams told me. "They sound old and weak as old age approaches; they register pain and distress when injured. If anything modern is brought to their attention, such as an electric light, a radio, or an automobile, they are amazed and usually frightened."

Williams points out that it is out of the question to check most of the cases. "In this sort of work, however, the fact that something cannot be proven does not make it false. In many cases the subject will recount accurate details of things that he could not possibly know.

"Under hypnosis and regressed to a previous life, many subjects possess skills that are normally quite foreign to them, and often are lost arts.

"If, in a former life, the subject was literate and could write, I will ask him to write something for me. When I compare the handwriting of the previous personality with the script of the present personality, I am able to see that the two styles are completely different. While regressed, the hypnotized subject is reliving another life in every detail.

"One argument that is often raised is that there exists a blood relationship between the person today and the prior incarnation. It is then claimed that the subject is just recounting old family stories that he has heard long ago but forgotten.

"I have never found any blood relationship from life to life.

"There is also the argument that the subject may be telling about someone or something that he has read.

"In the case of 'Jonathan,' the previous personality was from a small town, unlikely ever to have been heard of by George Field. Jonathan Powell was an obscure, poor, uneducated farmer, who would never make the history books, although he may now!

"Another argument which is often raised against the reincarnation thesis is that the subject is only picking up a psychic record or image of one who has lived in the past and is not reliving his own past life.

"This can be accomplished through hypnosis, and I have done it. However, when this is done, the subject sees the people and events only as an observer, as if he were watching a movie. This is quite different from a regression to a subject's own previous life. When a subject is regressed, he *relives* the experiences which he describes.

"A phenomenon which can happen, and apparently does in some cases of spontaneous recall where the person has died recently and nearby, is the partial possession of a subject by a disincarnate spirit. This, of course, is considered to be nonsense by the materialists, but this belief was accepted by the early Christians. This is the reason cited for Jesus casting the demons into the herd of swine and then sending them on to drown."

I found correspondence with Loring G. Williams to be most fascinating and helpful in the gathering of material for this book. As for what his investigations prove, Williams says that perhaps each reader must decide for himself. The skeptic will proclaim that nothing has been proven, that there are no facts, only coincidences. The believer will proclaim that, at last, we have proof of reincarnation.

Williams has tried to remain objective but cannot resist the feeling that there is much more here than coincidence can account for. He believes that they found as much evidence for Jonathan as one could hope to find, after 100 years, of the life of someone who lived a short and unremarkable existence. He convinced Jonathan Powell *did* live in Jefferson, N.C., from 1834 to 1863. After knowing Jonathan and visiting Jefferson with him, Williams can believe nothing else.

BRIDEY MURPHY REVISITED

To a great number of Americans, "Bridey Murphy" has become synonymous with reincarnation. This story of the Pueblo, Colorado, housewife who remembered a past life while under hypnosis made a dramatic impact upon the public imagination. Newspapers, magazines, and scholarly journals debated the validity of the "memory," and the controversy surrounding this alleged case of reincarnation has not resolved itself to this day.

William J. Barker of the Denver *Post* published the first account of this now famous case in that newspaper's *Empire* magazine. Barker told how Morey Bernstein, a young Pueblo business executive, first noticed what an excellent subject "Mrs. S." was for deep trance when he was asked to demonstrate hypnosis at a party in October of 1952.

It was some weeks later, on the evening of November 29th, that Bernstein gained the woman's consent to participate in an experiment of age-regression.

The amateur hypnotist had heard stories of men who had led their subjects back into past lives, but he had always scoffed at such tales. He had been particularly skeptical about the testimony of the British psychiatrist, Sir Alexander Cannon, who reported that he had investigated over a thousand cases wherein entranced individuals had recalled past incarnations.

Mrs. S., who later became identified as Ruth Simmons, was not particularly interested in hypnotism nor in becoming a guinea pig for Bernstein's attempt to test the thesis of Cannon and the others who had claimed investigation of former lives. She was, at that time, 28 years old, an attractive young matron who enjoyed playing bridge and attending ball games with her husband. Mrs. S. was, to employ a Madison Avenue cliche, the typical American housewife.

With Mr. Simmons and Mrs. Bernstein as witnesses, the hypnotist began to lead Mrs. Simmons back through significant periods of her childhood. Finally, it was time for the big try.

Bernstein placed Mrs. Simmons in a trance, then told her that she was going back until she found herself in another time and another place. The hypnotist told his subject that she would be able to talk to him and tell him what she saw.

Bernstein paused for a glass of water, waited another minute or two before he spoke again to Mrs. Simmons.

When he asked her if she could view a scene from an earlier existence, the woman began to breathe heavily. Her first words from an alleged previous memory were more enigmatic than dramatic.

"I'm scratching the paint off my bed, because I'm mad. I had just got an awful spankin!"

When Bernstein asked for the personality's name and was told "Bridey Murphy," the strange search for evidence of a former incarnation had begun.

At first, though, the hypnotist-businessman was unimpressed with his subject's apparent memory of a former existence in Ireland, because "strange responses often come from people under hypnosis."

Then Bridey—short for Bridget—began to use words and expressions that were completely out of character for Mrs. Simmons. And, as Mr. Simmons pointed out, more than simply being out of character, the use of certain terms required a knowledge which his "ordinary" wife did not, nor could not, possess.

Bridey told of playing hide'n'seek with her brother Duncan, who had "reddish hair like mine" (Mrs. Simmons was a brunette).

She told of attending Mrs. Strayne's school in Cork where she spent her time "studying to be a lady."

With sensitivity she recreated her marriage to Brian MacCarthy, a young lawyer, who took her to live in Belfast in a cottage back of his grandmother's house, not far from St. Theresa's church.

In her melodic brogue, "Bridey Murphy" told of a life without children, a life laced with a small point of conflict because she was Protestant while Brian was Catholic, then, in a tired and querulous voice, she told them how she had fallen down a flight of stairs when she was 66.

After her fall, Bridey had had to be carried about.

The burden was lifted one Sunday when she died while Brian was at church. It upset him terribly, Bridey said. She recalled how she lingered beside her husband, trying to establish communication with him, trying to let him know that he should not grieve for her.

"People on earth won't listen," she complained.

Bridey told the astonished hypnotist and his witnesses that she had waited around Belfast until Father John, a priest friend of her husband's, had passed away. She wanted to point out to him that he was wrong about purgatory, she said, and added that he admitted it.

The spirit world, she said, was one in which you couldn't talk to anybody very long . . . they'd go away. One did not sleep, never ate, and never became tired. Bridey thought that she had lived in the spirit realm for about 40 years before she was reborn as Mrs. Simmons.

At a second session, Bridey again stressed that the "afterlife" was painless, nothing to be afraid of. There was neither love nor hate, and relatives did not stay together in clannish groups.

Her father, she recalled, said he saw her mother, but she didn't.

The spirit world, then, was simply a place where the soul waited to pass on to "another form of existence."

Details of Bridey Murphy's physical life on earth began to amass on Morey Bernstein's tape recorders. Business associates who heard the tapes encouraged Bernstein to continue with his experiments but to let someone else, a disinterested third party, check Bridey's statements in old Irish records or wherever such evidence might be found.

Ruth Simmons was not eager to continue with the series of experiments, but the high regard which both she and her husband had for Morey Bernstein led her to consent to submit to additional sessions.

Bernstein told *Empire* magazine that he made careful notes in preparation for each session after the personality of Bridey Murphy had revealed itself.

The hypnotist stressed the importance of avoiding loaded questions in dealing with an entranced person. The subject becomes child-like in that he will be disposed to say what he thinks the hypnotist wants him to say.

During each session, additional "evidence" of her existence was given to the researchers by the charming Irish woman.

She recalled how her mother had told her stories of the Irish Hercules, Cuchulain the warrior.

Utilizing the body of Mrs. Simmons, Bridey demonstrated a graceful and lively rendition of an Irish folk dance which she called "the Morning Jig." Her favorite songs were learned to be "Sean," "The Ministrel's March," and "The Londonderry Air." Mrs. Simmons had no interest in musical activities previously.

Barker asked Morey Bernstein if he felt the strange case of Bridey Murphy could be explained by memory which had been transferred through Mrs. Simmon's ancestors.

The young hypnotist-businessman conceded that the whole episode would make a better story if it could be proved that Bridey Murphy were one of Mrs. Simmons' forebears. The subject was one-third Irish, but the genetic memory hypothesis falls apart when it is remembered that Bridey had no children.

Other researchers who have regressed subjects back into previous life-memories have found that blood line and heredity have nothing to do with former incarnations. Many have spoken of the after-life as a kind of "stockpile of souls." When a particular type of spirit is required to inhabit and animate a body that is about to be born, that certain spirit is selected and introduced into that body.

Bernstein observed frankly and humorously that a person who boasts of having noble French ancestry may have been an African slave or a Chinese concubine on his last visit to the physical plane.

In Bernstein's opinion, one could only take one of two points of view in regard to the strange case of Bridey Murphy. One might conclude that the whole thing had been a hoax without a motive. This conclusion would hold that Mrs. Simmons was not the "normal young gal" she seemed to be, but actually a frustrated actress who proved to be a consummate performer in her interpretation of a script dreamed up by Morey Bernstein "because he likes to fool people."

If one were not to accept that particular hypothesis, Bernstein said, then the public must admit that the experiment may have opened a hidden door for just a second, and that, without fully understanding what had been seen, it had been an exciting glimpse of immortality.

Doubleday released Morey Bernstein's *The Search*

for Bridey Murphy in 1956. Bernstein claimed that he had invested $10,000 in his exploration of Bridey's assertion of a physical existence and that he did not hope to earn that much in royalties from sales of the book. Furthermore, the businessman stated, he did not care if his expenditures were met or not. He had, he hoped, opened up an important facet of man's existence for further exploration.

Skeptics and serious investigators alike were interested in testing Bernstein's thesis that Bridey Murphy had given America an "exciting glimpse of immortality."

In mid-January, 1956, the Chicago *Daily News* sent its London representative on a three-day safari into Ireland. He was assigned to check out Cork, Dublin, and Belfast and uncover any evidence which might serve as verification for the Bridey Murphy claims. With only one day for each city, it is not surprising that the newsman reported that he could find nothing of significance.

In February, the Denver *Post* sent William Barker, the man who first reported the story of the search for Bridey Murphy, to conduct a thorough investigation of the enigma. Barker felt that certain strong points had already been established by Irish investigators and had been detailed in Bernstein's book.

Bridey (Irish spelling of the name is Bridie) had said that her father-in-law, John MacCarthy had been a barrister (lawyer) in Cork. A lawyer in Dublin had written the book publishers on September 30, 1954 and informed them that there was a John MacCarthy from Cork, a Roman Catholic educated at Clongowes School, listed in the Registry of Kings Inn.

Bridie had mentioned a "green-grocer," John Carrigan with whom she had traded in Belfast. A Belfast librarian, in a letter dated May 19, 1955, had attested to the fact that there had been a man of that name and trade at 90 Northumberland during the time in which the personality of Bridie Murphy had claimed to have lived there.

The librarian, a Mr. John Bebbington, had also verified the personality's statement that there had been a William Farr who had sold foodstuffs during this same period.

One of the most significant bits of information had to do with a place that Bridey Murphy had called Mourne. Such a place was not shown on any modern maps of Ireland, but its existence was substantiated through the British Information Service.

While entranced, Ruth Simmons had "remembered" that Catholics could teach at Queen's University, Belfast, even though it was a Protestant institution. American investigators had made a hasty prejudgment when they learned of such a statement and had challenged the likelihood of such an interdenominational teaching arrangement. In Ireland, however, such a fact was common knowledge, and Bridey had scored another hit.

Barker conceded that any one of the items taken *separately* did not constitute proof of reincarnation. The newsman did feel, however, that all of the details combined did begin to add up into a most provocative case for the defense.

Then there were such things as Bridie knowing about the old Irish custom of dancing at weddings and putting money in the bride's pockets. There was also her familiarity with the currency of that period, the crops of the region, the contemporary musical pieces, and the folklore of the area.

When Barker dined with a hotel owner who was interested in the "search," the newsman questioned Bridie's referring to certain food being prepared in "flats."

Flats wasn't a word we knew in that context, Barker told his host, Kenneth Besson.

Besson waved a waiter to their table and asked him to bring some flats.

When the waiter returned, Barker saw that flats were like platters, far as he could see. It was a perfectly normal term there, Besson said.

Several scholars had felt that Bridie had committed a gross error when she mentioned the custom of kissing the Blarney Stone.

The Blarney superstition was a comparatively late 19th century notion, Dermot Foley, the Cork city librarian told Barker.

Later Foley told the reporter that he owed Bridie an apology. T. Crofton Cronker, in his *Researches in the South of Ireland,* 1824, mentions the custom of kissing the Blarney stone as early as 1820.

But Bridie Murphy did not always score. Numerous Irish historians and scholars felt that she must have been more Scottish than Irish. They were especially firm about the name Duncan, which she had given for that of her father and her brother.

"I wonder if she might have been tryin' to say Dunnock instead of Duncan," speculated John Collins, described as a "walking history book" of Irish customs.

On Barker's long flight home to Denver, he tried to organize his conclusions. Later, he published the findings of his own private search for Bridey Murphy in the *Post.*

On the debit side, Bridey had been wrong about most of her people, even about alleged facts in her own life. Barker had been unable to find complete birth data on either Bridey or her kin. The personality had used the word "barrister" with a frequency that amazed educated Irishmen. And Bridey had shocked most Irishmen with her crude term, "ditched" to describe her burial. Barker was told that the Irish are much too reverent toward the dead to employ such a brutal word.

The personality, speaking through Mrs. Simmons, had demonstrated little knowledge of Ireland's history from 1800 to the 1860's. Bridey and Brian's honeymoon route had become hopelessly untraceable and confused with the trip she had made to Antrim as a child of 10. The principal difficulty in accepting Bridey's story lay in the fact that so much of the testimony was untraceable and unverifiable.

On the credit side of Bridey Murphy's ledger were all the many things which she had been right about, even though the scholars and the authorities at first stated that she was wrong.

There was the matter of the iron bed which she had scratched with her fingernails. Certain authorities discredited this statement on the grounds that iron beds had not yet been introduced into Ireland during the period in which Bridey had claimed to live. The *Encyclopaedia Brittanica,* however, states that iron beds did appear in Bridey's era and were advertised as being "free from the insects which sometimes infected wooden bedsteads."

Extremely convincing is Bridey's vocabulary. If the whole thing were nothing other than an elaborate hoax, Ruth Simmons must rate as one of the most brilliant character actresses of all time. One of the most difficult things to attain in achieving a convincing characterization is the speech pattern of the person being mimed. Our speech patterns are as distinctive as our fingerprints. The personality of Bridey Murphy never faltered in her almost poetic speech, and of the hundreds of words of jargon and colloquial phrases which she uttered, nearly all were found to be just right for the time in which she claimed to have lived. The songs which Bridey sang, her graphic word pictures of wake and marriage customs were all acclaimed by Irish folklorists as being accurate.

Her grim reference to the "black something" which took the life of her baby brother probably referred to famine or disease. The Irish use of "black" in this manner means "malignant" and would have nothing to do with the actual color of the pestilence.

Barker found that Bridey had bested the authorities on several occasions. Bridey's claims to have eaten muffins as a child, to have obtained books from a lending library in Belfast, to have known about the Blarney stone were, at first, judged to be out of proper time context. Later, her challengers actually uncovered historical substantiation for the statements made by Bridey through Ruth Simmons.

What did he think about the whole Bridey business? Barker wrote. It was no fraud, he said, whatever it was. And it wasn't telepathy.

Certain researchers of psychic phenomena have disagreed with this analysis. While agreeing that the Bridey Murphy case is not a *consciously* contrived fraud, many investigators will not rule out the role that telepathy or some other extrasensory ability may have played in the "memory" of the Irish housewife.

First of all, one must concede that certain items could have been "remembered" by the Colorado housewife via normal means and could have been dug out of her subconscious by the hypnotic trance induced by Morey Bernstein. "Mrs. S." could have had several acquaintances throughout her childhood who were familiar with Ireland and who may have each imparted a bit of the memory of "Bridey Murphy."

Many skeptical researchers tried to apply the phenomenon of cryptomnesia to Ruth Simmons (later disclosed to be Mrs. Virginia Tighe), who was adopted in infancy by her mother's sister, a woman with the typical mixed heritage of the average American. Cryptomnesia holds that a child might somehow have known a person who relayed the information which he later seemed to remember about a previous life. The child would have forgotten both the source of his "memory" and the fact that he had ever obtained it, although he would remember the information so that he might dramatically present it as recalled from a past incarnation. The attempts to discredit Bridey Murphy as a manifestation of cryptomnesia fail in the estimation of researchers C. J. Ducasse and Ian Stevenson. In Stevenson's estimation, the critics of the Bridey Murphy case provided only suppositions of possible sources of information, not evidence that these had been the sources.

It cannot be denied that Bridey possessed a knowledge of 19th century Ireland which contained a number of items of information which were unfamiliar even to authorities and historians. Such details, when checked after elaborate research, were found to be correct in Bridey's favor.

It is when the reader finds himself up against these annoying "hits" that cannot be undermined by the most penetrating analysis that he finds himself forced to admit that "Mrs. S.," alias Bridey Murphy, either acquired the information paranormally (i.e. through extrasensory means) or by reliving the memory of a past life.

REINCARNATION—OR A VOICE FROM BEYOND?

The voice spoke in a slow drawl. "Hope I'm not intrudin', but my name is Dave Dean. I'm a Kentuckian, a 'long hunter,' and the Shawnees scalped me!"

In the late fall of 1946 and on into 1947, author and psychic researcher Edmond P. Gibson attended a series of sittings with William H. Thatcher, a trance medium, in Grand Rapids, Michigan.

According to Gibson, the spirit personality which manifested did more toward proving survival and contributing to historical knowledge than Bridey Murphy dreamed of.

Speaking through Thatcher, the spirit voice told of being born in the 1760's, having lived for a time in Boonesboro, and being a member of George Rogers Clark's expedition to Kaskaskia. Many of the names which the medium relayed for Dave Dean were easily found and substantiated. Some of the facts and incidents which the spirit voice cited were at first thought to be totally incorrect. Extensive research in dusty old tomes proved that Dave Dean had been right. Although Dean was never too clear about his dates, he remembered details that seemed to be genuine memories of a physical existence in the frontier America of 1760 to 1800.

Even some of the most obscure items which Dave Dean mentioned were later found to be historically correct. Attempts to trip the spirit of the frontiersman most often ended with a victory for Dave Dean.

Having Clark's memoirs of the expedition available, Gibson noted that on the march to Vincennes, the troops were frequently in water to their armpits. In his last sitting with the Thatcher seance circle, Gibson asked Dave what song the men sang as they marched to Vincennes.

The voice said they didn't do much marching, but were wading in water up to their waists most of the time.

Dave Dean cited "Lil Ol' Bolero" and "World Turned Upside Down" as two favorite songs of the men.

The investigators found that a song entitled *Lillibullero*, written about 1766, had been very popular both among British soldiers and the frontiersmen. The original Spanish words were quickly corrupted on the frontier, and the lyrics were sung phonetically and with gusto by the backwoodsmen. It is easy to see how *Lillibullero* became "Lil Ol' Bolero" under such conditions of performance.

So it may have been with "World Turned Upside Down." In the *Journal of the American Society for Psychical Research* for July, 1950, Dave Dean recalled as much as he could of the lyrics of this marching song:

> "I've traveled far and I've traveled wide
> In every port and clime,
> (Here he says he forgets some of it.)
> I've drunk my lot, I've filled my shot
> In country and in town
> 'Till I got a wife.
> An' the world turned upside down."

The names of the men whom Dean designated as especially lusty singers were found on the roster of the First Virginia Dragoons, but the song itself was not easily traced. Then, finally, a researcher uncovered an 18th Century Marching song:

> "When I was young and in my prime,
> I'd neither thought nor care,
> I took delight in mirth and wine
> And rov'd from fair to fair:
> I took delight in jovial life,
> 'Til fate on me did frown:
> Until alas! I got a wife,
> And the world turned upside down."

They discovered that this march-time ballad was very popular among the British soldiers during the Revolution. Again, it is quite easy to see how homespun frontiersmen could have rearranged the lyrics in their version of, "The World Turned Upside Down."

The communication of Dave Dean through the medium Thatcher fills 40 single spaced, typewritten pages. The entire transcript was sent to a nationally known historian, R. E. Banta, whose special interest in American history has been the Ohio River Valley.

"I not only 'care to look over' Dave Dean's communications, but I have read them through three times," Banta wrote the researchers. "This is one of the most interesting documents I've seen.

"Thatcher's subconscious is out, mainly. I have stowed away a great deal more information about the Ohio frontier than he can know exists and no one could call up any such volume as this, on short notice, out of my dormant cells.

". . . This thing could open up an entirely new field of historical research but it would surely catch hell from the 'union members' in the process!"

Although the possibility of the medium having extrasensory access to existing literary sources must be one of the hypotheses considered, many of the investigators favored the theory that an authentic communication from the dead had been received.

Might such communication from "beyond the grave" explain all cases of reincarnation? Could it be that those who claim memories of past lives have become unwilling mediums and have been temporarily controlled by another personality? This possession could last for but the duration of the period of mediumistic or hypnotic trance, or it might last for several months, as in the case of Mary Roff-Lurancy Vennum.

"Mother. I heard voices in my room last night. Voices that called out 'Rancy, Rancy,' and it was as if I could feel someone's breath on my face."

Such was the beginning of a marked change in the life of Lurancy Vennum, a life that had been quite normal and uneventful up until that morning in 1877.

Mary-Lurancy Vennum—Rancy, as she was called by her family—was born on April 16, 1864 to James J. Vennum and his wife Lurinda, near the town of Watseka, Illinois. It was in her thirteenth year that the strange occurrences began to take place.

On July 11, 1877, Lurancy began to have recurring fits, sometimes several a day, often times lapsing into unconsciousness. Sometimes she became quite violent and had to be restrained. At other times, she lay, almost corpse-like as if entombed in the ether of some nether world.

The trances, which lasted something over six months, had varied effects on the young girl. At times she experienced pain and agony; on other occasions she seemed to approach ecstasy. She spoke of heaven and angels and of contact with the deceased.

Word of Lurancy's problem attracted more than a passing interest from A. B. Roff, a highly respected citizen in the community of Watseka. His daughter, Mary, had undergone similar fits years earlier and had subsequently died from one of them.

Because of his past experience, Mr. Roff sympathized greatly with the Vennums and was finally able to persuade Mr. Vennum to allow him and an acquaintance, Dr. E. W. Stevens, to come to the Vennum home to observe Lurancy. Dr. Stevens was a Wisconsin physician and prominent psychical researcher. He was familiar with the case of Roff's daughter, Mary, and hence greatly interested in another case so close, bearing such similarities.

When Roff and Stevens arrived at the Vennum residence on January 31, 1878, Lurancy was sitting near a stove in a deep trance.

At this time she claimed to be a 63-year-old woman, Katrina Hogan. Later Katrina seemed to fade into Willie Cunning, a wayward youngster who had passed away.

Getting nowhere with Lurancy's constant changing of identity, Dr. Stevens suggested to her that the spirits that controlled her might send someone more rational and intelligent so that she might have more control over herself. Lurancy replied that there were many who would like to come, and she proceeded to name a list of people who had been dead for quite some time, and who, in life, she, as Lurancy, had never known.

When Lurancy had finished recounting the eerie roster of souls, she said, "But there is one whom the angels have chosen . . . Mary Roff. She will come."

Roff was overcome with excitement. "Oh yes, let her come!" he said, thinking of his daughter who had died twelve years before.

When Lurancy awoke the next morning, she recognized none of the Vennums. She insisted that she was Mary Roff and begged her "father" (Roff) to take her home. Roff was dissuaded from such a move and Mary-Lurancy remained with the Vennums.

A short while later, Mary's mother and sister were on their way to the Vennum home to see Mary-Lurancy. Upon seeing the two relatives Lurancy embraced them and called her sister by the pet name 'Nervie,' which only Mary Roff had ever used.

This confrontation seemed to make the child even more homesick than before, so a move was agreed upon, and on February 11, 1878, "Mary" was allowed to go to the Roff home and stay.

During her sojourn in the Roff home, "Mary" recognized every person that she had known while she had been alive, from twelve to twenty-five years before. Lurancy-Mary also recalled many incidents which had occurred while she was still alive. The girl never seemed to recognize the Vennums until after they had made several trips to visit her and the two families had become close friends.

Then, in May of that same year, the girl told Mrs. Roff that Lurancy Vennum was coming back. "Mary" closed her eyes as if being led into a trance-like state, then the change took place.

When the Lurancy personality emerged, she looked around and asked where she was. Mrs. Roff told her, and the distressed girl asked to be taken to her home. The transformation had only lasted for a few minutes when Lurancy again left and the Mary personality returned.

One of the most interesting incidents in the dual life of Lurancy-Mary occurred one afternoon when she stated that her brother, Frank Roff, should be carefully watched, for that evening he would become gravely ill and might possibly die if proper attention were not available. Frank, at the time, appeared quite healthy.

Dr. Stevenson checked with the family that night and then proceeded on to a patient's house in "Old Town." It was expected that that was where he would spend the night, but for some reason, he returned, unannounced, to the Roff neighborhood to stay at a Mrs. Marsh's.

At about two A.M. Frank went into convulsions.

"Go get Dr. Stevens," cried Lurancy-Mary. "He's at Mrs. Marsh's."

"No," the family argued, "he's in 'Old Town.'"

"He's at Mrs. Marsh's," the girl insisted, and indeed, that is where the physician was found.

When Dr. Stevens arrived on the scene, he found Mary already treating her brother. She seemed to be doing everything quite properly, so he allowed her to continue under his guidance.

As time passed, the personalities occasionally attempted to alternate, the Mary dominance receding, permitting Lurancy to come through faintly. The changes were never complete enough to either totally obliterate the Mary personality or permit a full manifestation of the Lurancy personality.

Then one day Mary became quite disconsolate. "Lurancy is coming back," she said, and she gave a date and time.

The Mary personality immediately set about getting ready to leave, bidding farewell to friends and relatives. On the prescribed day, she and Mr. Roff were on their way to the Vennum house when the transformation took place. Upon arriving at her own home, Lurancy recognized all of the members of her family and seemed to show no ill effects from her experience.

On January 11, 1882, Lurancy married a farmer, George Binning. The Roffs visited her frequently, both before and after her marriage, and up until the time when she and her husband moved farther west in 1884.

In a letter to the *Religio-philosophical Journal*, Mr. Roff wrote that, for a time, "Mary" would take control of Lurancy for brief periods and then recede again. "Aside from this, she had little opportunity of using her mediumship, her parents being afraid to converse with her on the subject lest it should cause a return of the 'spells' . . . and her husband never made himself acquainted with spiritualism. . . ."

"She has never had any occasion for a physician since she left us, never having been sick since then. . . . With the birth of her first child, Lurancy became entranced, and did not recover consciousness until after the child was born."

Later, psychical researchers made attempts to get some statements directly from Mrs. Lurancy Binning, but no answer to the inquiries was ever received.

Perhaps in the case of Lurancy Vennum we might find a model case study of temporary possession and use it as a guide by which we might distinguish between cases of possession and cases suggestive of reincarnation.

To briefly summarize the case, we recall that Mary Roff had died when Lurancy was but fifteen months old. Although the two families lived in the same town, they were only slightly acquainted. During the period in which the Mary personality possessed Lurancy, she not only displayed the personal characteristics of Miss Roff, but she exhibited a knowledge of Mary's life which would have been quite beyond the capacity of either Lurancy or her parents. The Roffs themselves were convinced that their daughter had returned in the body of Miss Vennun. One knows how readily eager-to-believe parents might be momentarily deceived in the dim light of a seance room, but the Roffs were able to live with "Mary" for a period of several months. At no time did she falter in her knowledge of incidents and people with which she would have been acquainted as Mary Roff.

And at no time did "Mary" claim to be a past life of Lurancy Vennum. "Mary" had temporarily returned in Lurancy Vennum's body, and she spoke of Miss Vennum as a separate and distinctly different personality. (The same thing was true in the Dave Dean communications. At no time did the frontiersman claim to be a previous life of William Thatcher, the medium.)

This element of behavior on the part of the surviving or communicating personality seems to offer the investigator the principal difference between temporary possession and cases suggestive of reincarnation. At no time, in cases where the percipient of the experience seems truly to recall a prior life, does another personality claim to be utilizing the body of the percipient as means of communication. In true cases suggestive of reincarnation, the percipient claims to remember how he once felt and reacted to his environment in a previous life.

A case similar to that of Mary Roff-Lurancy Vennum, in which a separate personality controlled or possessed the body of the percipient, is that of Iris Farczady, a 15-year-old girl in Budapest, who seemed to have been "reborn" as a Spanish charwoman.

"Iris is dead," Mrs. Farczady told Cornelius Tabori, a well-known psychic investigator, when he arrived for an interview with the family in 1933. "She left us in August. She who lives with us now is called Lucia—a woman from Madrid."

Mr. Farczady was a chemical engineer. His wife was the daughter of a distinguished Viennese officer. Such a respected family as the Farczadys would seem to have nothing to gain and much to lose by attempting to perpetrate a hoax.

Mrs. Farczady told Tabori that she had always prided herself on being an enlightened, level-headed woman. Her daughter, Iris, had been a brilliant pupil—an outstanding mathematician and linguist, who had studied French and German.

"Then, that night in August, she felt ill. I put her to bed and sat with her. Suddenly she gave a long sigh. Somehow I knew that my darling, clever daughter had died.

"I bent over to listen to her heart; it was still beating. But I was right. My daughter had died. The person who had taken her body awoke, shouting in some foreign tongue. We tried to calm her, but she did not understand us. She jumped from the bed and tried to run from the house. She kept mentioning Pedro and Madrid. At last we realized that she was speaking Spanish."

Try as the family would to communicate with Iris, she would speak only Spanish. She could neither understand nor speak a single word of Hungarian, French or German. It took the concentrated efforts of the large Farczady clan to teach her enough German so that they might be able to converse with her.

Tabori addressed Iris in German and received an angry protest because he had not called her by her "real" name.

"My name is Lucia Salvio," she corrected him in her heavily accented German. During the interview, she explained to the investigator that she had felt very ill that August afternoon in Madrid. Her husband, Pedro, had been away at work. When Lucia realized that she was dying, her first concern had been for her fourteen children—one for each year of her married life.

Mrs. Farczady commented to Tabori on the great diversity of temperament between her serious, studious Iris and the gay Lucia, who sang and danced for them.

"When I first looked into the mirror after coming here, I was shocked," Lucia-Iris told the researcher. "I wondered what had happened to me and where my black eyes and thick dark hair had gone. Now I find it quite pleasing that in my new life, I am such a lovely young girl. My only regret is for my poor motherless children."

To seek substantiation for the bizarre story from a member outside of the immediate family circle, Tabori later visited Dr. Tibor Huempfner, a Cistercian professor who had spent many years in Madrid. The professor remarked that he had been astonished when the girl spoke Spanish to him and described the churches of Madrid in great detail. Huempfner had also been present at a party where Iris-Lucia had amazed a Spanish teacher by speaking to him in a perfect Madrid dialect.

The case of Concetto Buonsignore is also one of such complete possession by a controlling entity that the percipient lost his ability to speak in his native tongue.

Buonsignore, a Sicilian peasant, awoke one morning speaking ancient Greek in the voice of one who had been dead for 2,700 years. Again, at no time, did the "voice" claim to be recalling a previous existence of the simple farmer.

Thinking that her husband had been overtaken by a spirit, or at the very least become insane, his wife motioned for him to follow her, and she led him to the priest of the small Sicilian town. The peasants, who greeted him along the way, were astounded to hear him babble back unintelligbly, as if he did not know them at all. After a moment's concern, they shrugged it off as the after effects of the previous evening's festival.

After listening to the man, the priest realized that he was not simply mouthing meaningless prattle. "Your husband is speaking in some strange language," he informed the wife of Buonsignore.

"What language?" the wife asked with a scowl. "He's never been off Sicily!"

But the priest was convinced that the old peasant farmer was speaking in some unfamiliar tongue. He sent for Father B., stationed in Palermo, who was a professor of literature, and had great facility with languages. The priest came to Pergusa and listened carefully as Concetto Buonsignore spoke.

The linguist immediately announced that the man was speaking in Greek—though it was a variety of a very ancient dialect that the scholar had only come across in the Greek of Homer and his contemporaries.

After listening for a while longer, Father B. came to the astonishing conclusion that the Sicilian peasant was reliving a personality that was 27 centuries old!

The first time that Concetto Buonsignore had even heard of Greece was when his son was sent to that country with an expeditionary force of the Italian army in World War II. But, as the Sicilian spoke to Father B., he described the surroundings and the times of the ancient city of Athens.

His house, he claimed, was in front of the altar and the temple of Demeter, and the dwelling was shaded by a large tree. He described a distinguished military career in which he had fought for his city-state as a soldier and a sailor. The priest was able to identify one of the battles in which he had taken part as the battle of Aegospotami in 405 B.C.!

The "voice" went on to describe in correct detail how the Athenians had lost the naval battle by not heeding the words of Alcibiades, and how, the following year, Sparta had been able to dissolve the Athenian empire because of the loss of the fleet.

Concetto Buonsignore quickly became a celebrity, and newsmen began to converge on the island of Sicily and on the town of Pergusa.

The journal *La Domenica del Corriere* did print a long article reviewing the strange manifestation in its December 29, 1946 issue. The Milan reporter was one of the few who had arrived in time to hear the peasant use the ancient Greek tongue.

On the fifth day of possession, the personality of the ancient Greek sailor left the body of Buonsignore as suddenly as it had come. The last words spoken in the ancient tongue were directed at his wife: "I feel hungry." From that time on, the peasant lapsed back into his original personality and to the Sicilian dialect that he had spoken from birth.

The actual conversations that occurred between the Pergusa priest and the peasant farmer, while Buonsignore was in the entranced state, were recorded, witnessed, notarized, and filed with the French Academy of Sciences in Paris. The language professor, Father B., called in from Palermo, also signed the document as a witness.

And then there are those who voluntarily offer themselves as temporary physical dwellings for those who have "passed over." Especially in the phenomenon known as spirit healing do we find individuals who allow their bodies to be possessed by the alleged spirits of deceased physicians so that the great healers' work might be continued.

Dona Silvina, one of Portugal's most well-known witches, receives more than 100 clients a day. Her tiny house sometimes becomes so crowded that apprentice witches distribute numbered cards at the entrance, supermarket style, and Dona Silvina treats patients in groups of five.

Several pairs of crutches hang on the wall in silent testimony to the cripples who have been cured after a visit to the 20th century witch. Dozens of letters from grateful patients swell the files of this most unusual clinic.

The portly witch takes no credit for herself. "Everything that I give comes from my hands. They transmit the good wishes of the good doctor, Dr. Sousa Martins."

Dr. Sousa Martins died 70 years ago after a life of unselfish work among the poor people of Portugal. Dona Silvina claims that she allows the spirit of the doctor to "incarnate" within her and to use her body as an instrument by which he might continue his ministry of healing.

Dona Silvina invokes the incarnation of Dr. Sousa Martins by repeating a set speech: "Let us thank our brother, Dr. Sousa Martins, for the cures he is about to give us."

Once the invocation has been uttered, the witch goes into convulsions near her altar. The patients who have come to seek the curative gifts of the spirit doctor also begin to writhe about on rugs which have been scattered on the floor.

When the spirit has arrived to possess the witch, Dona Silvina sits on a low chair beside her creaky iron bed. From deep within her throat comes a manly growl which is allegedly Dr. Sousa Martins' voice.

"I miss the earth," the voice tells those assembled. "I miss my sick patients."

Once incarnated in the ample flesh of Dona Silvina, the spirit of the doctor wastes little time. At once, he sets about prescribing healing rituals and calling forth various patients to be cured.

For those patients who claim to have benefited from the bizarre clinic of Dona Silvina, it matters little that they have allegedly been treated by a doctor who has been dead for over 70 years.

A MOST UNUSUAL FAMILY

The lovely Maria Januaria de Oliveiro was dying. At the entrance of her close friend, Ida Lorenz, she managed a slight smile. "Thank God you came in time," Maria said.

"Hush with that kind of talk, Sinha," Mrs. Lorenz said, using Maria's nickname. "You will soon be well."

Maria began a grim chuckle that ended in a painful spasm of coughing. When she had regained control, she said, "See there, the lungs are too far gone. I have planned it all rather well."

Ida Lorenz shook her head sadly. It was common knowledge among the Oliveiro family and their close friends that Sinha had deliberately exposed herself to the cold, damp weather. She had contracted a severe infection of her lungs and larynx which quickly developed into tuberculosis.

"I have planned it all," Sinha acknowledged, as if she could read her friend's thoughts. "I wanted to die."

"But why Sinha?" Ida Lorenz asked, no longer making an effort to check the tears that had begun to well in her eyes. "The beautiful daughter of a wealthy rancher in Rio Grande do Sul, you had everything to live for."

"I shall tell you why, my friend," Sinha gasped. "Let us start with the men who loved me, but who were driven away from my side by my disapproving father. One man even committed suicide because of me!

"In spite of my wealth, I have been lonely out here away from city life. My only happiness has been my visits to the village of Dom Feliciano to visit with you and your husband. You are a good woman, Ida Lorenz, and that is why I have planned my death so well."

Ida frowned. "I—I don't understand."

"I am going to come back as your daughter, Ida," Sinha said, a fierce intensity strengthening the wispy timbre of her voice. "I shall be reborn into your family. I shall be the child of Ida Lorenz, wife of F. V. Lorenz, village schoolmaster. I know that my next incarnation shall be a happy one!"

On August 14, 1918, ten months after the death of Sinha de Oliveiro, Ida Lorenz gave birth to a daughter, Marta. When the child was two and a half years old, she began to recall events in her life as Sinha.

Her older sister, Lola, was the first to report Marta's strange conversation of a time "when she was big."

It began that day when Marta beseeched her sister to carry her on her back. "You have legs of your own to walk on," Lola scowled. "There is no need for me to carry you."

Marta's lower lip quivered in a pout. "When you

were small and I was big, I used to carry you often enough!"

Lola laughed at her young sister's remark. "When were you ever bigger than you are now, little peanut?"

"When I lived with my other parents with the cows, oxen, and oranges on the ranch," Marta replied promptly.

Lola repeated Marta's humorous remark to her schoolmaster father. Mr. Lorenz smiled and gently told the child that they had never lived on a ranch.

"I don't mean you," Marta said. "I had other parents in those days."

"And did you have a little native servant like we have?" one of Marta's other sisters teased.

"No," Marta replied after a moment's thought. "Our servant was big. We did have a little native boy, though, and one day Father beat him for forgetting to fetch water from the well."

"Marta!" Mr. Lorenz said sternly. "I have never beaten a servant."

"I am speaking of my other father," Marta sighed impatiently. "And all the time my other father was beating him, the little boy kept shouting, 'Sinha, help me!' "

Mr. Lorenz was visibly taken aback by Marta's identifying herself with Sinha de Oliveiro. Neither he nor his wife had ever discussed Sinha's deathbed promise to return as their daughter, in front of the children. From that day on, the Lorenz children would be made increasingly familiar with the fact that their sister Marta claimed to have been among them before as "Maria-something-or-other-Oliveiro, but call me Sinha."

Marta made over 120 declarations of her life as Sinha, and each of these declarations was duly recorded and verified by her father.

She often expressed favoritism toward her brother, Carlos, and protested violently whenever she thought that other members of the Lorenz family might be mistreating him. When asked why she felt so protective toward her older brother, she reminded them that she (Sinha) had been Carlo's godmother.

When she was a child, her remembrances were usually prefaced with the phrase, "When I was big," but as she grew older she became more direct and recounted episodes in her previous life by beginning, "When I was Sinha."

Once during a rainstorm, one of the Lorenz children began to sob about a deceased sister, Emilia. "She will get wet down in her grave," the child worried.

Marta comforted her sibling by telling her that Emilia was not in the graveyard at all. "She is in a much better place than the one we are in," Marta said. "Her soul will always be safe."

Marta ceased being obsessed with her alleged life as Sinha when she was between the ages of seven and ten. She continued to speak of her former incarnation and her memory remained vivid, but she had begun to adjust to life as a member of the Lorenz family. After all, that had been Sinha's wish, to return as the daughter of her friend, Ida.

Mr. Lorenz did not inform Mr. de Oliveiro of his daughter's supposed rebirth until Marta was twelve. Mrs. de Oliveiro was never told of Sinha's alleged return.

Marta Lorenz grew up, married, and had a family of her own. In 1962, when she was interviewed by Dr. Ian Stevenson, Marta was living in Porto Alegre. She told the investigator that she had not forgotten her life as Sinha. Her death from tuberculosis remained particularly vivid in her memory of the former incarnation.

One reincarnation in a family would seem to be more than enough, but the F. V. Lorenz household hosted *two* children who claimed prior lives.

In October of 1921, the sister Emilia committed suicide by taking cyanide. She had been the second child and eldest daughter of the Lorenz family. She had been born in 1902 and had been given the name Emilia after Emilio, the Lorenz' first child, a boy, who had died in infancy.

According to the family, Emilia had not been happy as a girl and had repeatedly told members of the Lorenz household that if there were anything to the doctrine of reincarnation, she would return as a man. She rejected all proposals of marriage and made a number of suicide attempts before she swallowed the dose of cyanide.

Sometime after the death of Emilia, Mrs. Lorenz was given a spirit message while taking part in a seance. "Mamma, I will come as your son," said a voice she recognized as that of her deceased daughter. "Take me as your son."

Ida Lorenz was most skeptical about the spirit's plan for return, as she had already borne twelve children, of whom the youngest was the then three-year-old Marta, who claimed to be her deceased friend, Sinha. The spirit, however, was willing, and regardless of how weak the flesh may have supposed itself, Mrs. Lorenz did conceive for the thirteenth time. A little less than a year and a half after Emilia's suicide, she gave birth to a boy, whom the Lorenz' gave the name Emilio.

In Emilio, or Paulo, as he preferred, the reincarnated spirit seemed to become just a bit confused. If he were indeed Emilia returned as a boy, he should have been a rugged-type fellow who enjoyed being a boy. Emilia had, after all, given her dissatisfaction with her lot as a girl as the principal reason for her suicide. But Paulo steadfastly refused to wear boy's clothing, preferred to play with girls and dolls, gave evidence of an extraordinary talent for sewing, and identified himself with the deceased Emilia.

At last, when he was five, Paulo accepted a pair of trousers, which had been made out of a skirt belonging to the deceased Emilia, and this act seemed to bring about an increased acceptance of his sex role. Even as a grown man, however, (Dr. Stevenson was also able to interview Paulo during his visit to Brazil in 1962) Paulo Lorenz maintained an exceptionally strong identification with the feminine personality. He had never married and did, in fact, shun the company of women. It appears, then, that Emilia, if she did return, had taken that dose of cyanide in vain. Life as a man was obviously not the answer to her distress in the previous incarnation.

Our unusual family in Brazil opens up a most interesting point of speculation. We do not at our present level of scientific inquiry and knowledge know the limitations of genetic transmission. Neither do we know how much the mind of the mother can affect the development of the gestating child she carries in her womb. Mrs. Ida Lorenz is the common factor in both of these cases suggestive of reincarnation. Could she have been able, in some as yet unknown manner, to have forced the identification of Marta with Sinha and of Paulo with Emilia by impressing this suggestion on the minds of her unborn children?

THE MYSTERY OF NAOMI HENRY

In March, 1956, Henry Blythe, a professional hypnotist, was commissioned by the London *Daily Express* to undertake a duplication of Morey Bernstein's experiments with "Bridey Murphy."

As his subject in the experiment, Blythe chose Mrs. Naomi Henry, a 32-year-old housewife from Exeter.

Mrs. Henry, the mother of four children, had proved to be an exceptionally good subject in past demonstrations. She went under hypnosis rapidly, entered an unusually deep trance state, and was very sensitive to Blythe's suggestions and commands.

In an early series of experiments with Mrs. Henry, Blythe felt that he had been able to project her astral self from her body and accomplish remarkable feats of telepathy.

In his book, *The Three Lives of Naomi Henry,* Blythe wrote that he had succeeded in taking Naomi's 'self,' 'soul' or 'spirit' out of her physical body. If he could reproduce this phenomenon before an audience, he would be in a position to prove that the 'self' can leave the body and that therefore physical death need not be the end of everything because it was possible for the 'self' to exist outside the human envelope which encased it.

According to Blythe, he and Naomi succeeded wonderfully well in their demonstrations before large audiences at St. Mary's Bay holiday camp, Brixham. Blythe did, however, note that Naomi seemed exhausted after each performance and called for several glasses of water. The hypnotist became concerned for the woman's health, as did her husband, and Blythe ceased to use Mrs. Henry as a subject in 1951.

But now, five years later, there was a new challenge. The *Daily Express* had offered £250 for evidence of an authentic case of reincarnation in Britain. Blythe had accomplished age regression with several subjects, and he felt that if any one could recall a former life under hypnosis, as in the Bridey Murphy case, it would be Mrs. Naomi Henry.

On the afternoon of March 28, 1956, in the presence of four reporters, Blythe regressed Mrs. Henry as far back as her memory would go. The subject was commanded to tell those assembled who she was and what she was.

After a pause, her voice softly acknowledged that she was "Mary."

During that first session, Naomi-Mary told the hypnotist and the representatives of the press that she was a 17-year-old Irish farmgirl from Cork named Mary Cohen (because of this unusual surname for an Irish family, the name was thought, perhaps, to be Coen, Cowen, or Cowan—names which would sound the same as Cohen when spoken). Naomi-Mary recalled that the farm on which she lived was called Greengates, that the nearest village was Grener, and that her greatest affection was directed toward her 15-year-old brother, Sean.

The newspapermen were greatly impressed with Blythe's initial success and greatly urged him to attempt to discover more details of the Mary-life during the next session.

It was because of their insistence that Blythe try to learn the details of Mary's death that a most terrible and frightening thing occurred during that next experiment.

Blythe had begun by taking Naomi-Mary back to her life at age 27. By this time, "Mary" had been married to a man named Gaul, whom she did not love, and had had two sons. When Blythe progressed the personality to age fifty, the hypnotist and the assembled witnesses noted the physiological change which seemed to come over Mrs. Henry. A pained expression distorted her features; her mouth pulled down at the corners; and she looked older. Her attitude was one of bitterness toward a brutal husband who beat her and mistreated their sons.

Blythe moved Naomi-Mary up to age 60. At this stage, her speech became that of an old and senile woman. She was uncertain of her surroundings, vague about how old she was, and who was with her. She told Blythe that she was only able to hobble about on "sticks."

The hypnotist jumped ahead another ten years. The personality asked to lie down. Blythe assured her that she was lying down and need not fear.

He asked her how much longer she had to live.

Hoarsely the voice whispered that a woman said not long.

Then, after Blythe promised Naomi-Mary that things would soon be peaceful for her, the personality uttered, "Praise God!"

He was watching her closely, his fingers on the pulse on her left wrist, Blythe wrote of the session. Suddenly he felt her pulse die away, her breathing, clearly audible in the room during both sessions—stopped, every trace of color gone from her face. She appeared to be dead. He bent close to try and discover a trace of a breath, but there was nothing.

By urgently assuring Naomi-Mary that she was safe, Blythe managed to bring her out of the state of suspended animation into which she had entered.

Although Mrs. Henry bore no ill-effects from her five seconds of "death," the *Daily Express* chose to remove their support from the experiments at once. On April 28th, Donald Gomery wrote of his paper's decision to abandon the investigation.

Gomery related that a number of experiments across the whole of Britain, all conducted by professional hypnotists, had produced some most startling results. Then he mentioned the chilling episode which had taken place during Blythe's second session.

That woman, he pointed out, had "died" at 66. When the hypnotist asked what she was doing at 70 she realized that she was "dead." Then she stopped breathing.

That is why he felt the experiments should not continue— Because he now believed that there lay danger.

He confessed that when the report reached him, he felt more than frightened—he felt acutely afraid although the experiment was carried out by a professional hypnotist of known ability in front of witnesses. He was afraid that publication of such experiments might induce others, not sufficiently qualified, to carry out similar experiments without proper supervision, experiments that might have a damaging effect on the subject.

Blythe could not argue with the *Daily Express* decision. He felt that it was a blow to discontinue the investigation, but he could sympathize with the newspaper's position if even one amateur hypnotist were to regress even one person and possibly his heartbeats as a result of having read the series in the *Daily Express*.

To Blythe's great joy, however, Mrs. Henry agreed to continue the experiments privately.

On May 18th, in the hypnotist's consulting room, the investigation began its second session. Attending as witnesses were Mrs. Blythe, Dr. William C. Minifie, osteopath, Douglas Warner, author, and Elizabeth Warner, who was given the task of shorthand reporter. Although a tape recording was made of nearly all the sessions, Mrs. Warner's notes were useful both as a check against the tapes and as an ever-alert human record. The tape recorder needed to have its spools changed and might be "deaf" at a crucial moment.

Blythe brought Naomi back to her life as Mary Cohen and the investigators learned additional facts about the Irish girl's existence.

Her parents had literally given the bride away in marriage to Arthur Gaul.. Mary protested that she did not love her husband, but that her mother had told her that she couldn't keep her any longer.

The only pleasantness which Mary could remember

in her entire lifetime was the afternoons which she spent in the meadows with her younger brother, Sean.

Her death had come on the floor of an old house. Two or three old women and one old man had witnessed her death. Mary's last days were spent in pain, hobbling about on sticks, because her husband beat her so severely that he had broken a leg.

When Blythe asked her if she were glad to have finished that life, she answered, "Oh, yes!"

Then the hypnotist posed a question which each of the investigators had been eagerly awaiting: What happened to her in between that life when she was Mary Cohen and when she came back again to us . . . what was she doing in between that life and this?

Each member of the group leaned forward expectantly. Would they now hear details of what life was like after death? Would they at last be able to tell their fellow man what kind of existence he might expect beyond the grave?

"Nursing," came the answer.

The investigators shot one another bewildered glances. Blythe temporarily found himself at a loss for words. Her reply had been so totally unexpected that the hypnotist was forced to take a few moments to regain his control.

When he was once again able to direct his questions to the entranced subject, Blythe was startled to learn that he had uncovered yet another life of Naomi Henry.

In this life, the personality had been much happier. Her name had been Clarice Hellier, and she had been a nurse, who, at the turn of the century, had been responsible for the care of twenty-four children.

Clarice's life had been short and uneventful. She had died at 32 of a goiter in her throat, completely contented that her life had been spent caring for her wonderful children.

A crippled boy named Bobby had received the most attention from the nurse, and both Blythe and the other investigators noted the similarity between her love for Sean (in Mary's life) and her affection for the crippled Bobby. The comparison was brought into even sharper focus when the hypnotist regressed the personality back to Mary's life and they learned that Sean, too, had been a cripple!

During the fifth and last experiment, Naomi-Clarice was brought up to her time of death. She said she was at Westbury on Tyrm.

Blythe asked Clarice what she was doing at Westbury on Tyrm.

Clarice spoke slowly, squinting as if she were trying to read something which she could see but dimly. She hesitantly mentioned numbers, ending with the number two hundred and seven!

Blythe asked her what the number meant.

There was a long pause, and the investigators leaned forward to catch the faint, single word, *Grave.*

Clarice had been reading the number of her gravestone!

Then the voice was still. Blythe knew that this was the end of memory.

Gently the hypnotist spoke to Mrs. Henry and told her that the experiments were over. He assured her that he could take away every memory trace of what she had told them. She would go back to being her normal self. All memories of her previous existences would be wiped away, cleared from her mind and soul. She would come back to them as a normal, ordinary woman.

In the conclusion to his book, Blythe lists seven hypotheses which might explain the three lives of Naomi Henry: 1.) that he perpetrated an elaborate hoax to gain publicity for himself; 2.) that Naomi Henry managed an ingenious deception; 3.) that the subconscious mind of the hypnotist placed the deception into the subconscious of Mrs. Henry; 4.) that the hypnotist dredged up a compilation of strange memories from the subconscious of Mrs. Henry; 5.) that malignant spirits brought about the hoax; 6.) that the revelation of past lives is a gift from the spirit world to be used for mankind's enlightenment; 7.) that the experiments have proved reincarnation—that is, the re-birth after death of one spirit in the body of a new creation.

Blythe hopes that his reputation will serve to eliminate hypothesis number one from consideration. The hypnotist believes that Mrs. Henry must certainly be absolved. Not only does he consider the woman mentally and morally incapable of practicing a deliberate deception of such creative magnitude and histrionic ability, but he points out that even the greatest actress could not have stopped her pulse and breathing for five seconds and frightened a great newspaper into calling off so promising a series of investigations.

Blythe does give the third hypothesis its due, and he admits that Douglas Warner, the author who served as one of the witnesses, is inclined toward that particular explanation. The hypnotist personally rejects this theory, however, because he, in his experience, has "never known the subconscious to act so 'out of character.'" For the same reason, Blythe discards the fourth hypothesis.

As for the supernatural explanation postulated in the fourth and fifth theories, Blythe admits that he has no evidence to support spirit activity, but he concedes that such phenomena "may be possible."

The seventh hypothesis, that reincarnation is fact, Blythe feels may be supported by several confirming items which were subsequently uncovered by private investigators assigned to gather evidence of the physical existence of Mary Cohen and Clarice Hellier.

The hypnotist is most impressed by the fact that Mary-

Clarice-Naomi is recognizable through two centuries *as basically the same person*. If Naomi Henry had revealed an existence in 1790 as the daughter of a king, the whole story would have been less credible, while as Mary Cohen and Clarice Hellier there is an essential rightness which puts no strain on credulity.

It must have been this essential "rightness" which prompted Annie Besant to write (*The Ancient Wisdom*) that with reincarnation man is a dignified, immortal being, evolving towards a divinely glorious end; without it, he is a tossing straw on the stream of chance circumstances, irresponsible for his character, for his actions, for his destiny.

Do the three lives of Naomi Henry prove reincarnation with its evolution toward a "divinely glorious end?" Whatever hypothesis one wishes to accept at this point, the evidence amassed by Henry Blythe during the five sessions of hypnotically controlled regression must certainly be judged as most impressive. Whether the evidence offers substantial proof of reincarnation or another startling facet of mind, Blythe has made a great contribution toward the "final judgment."

WHOSE HAND GUIDED THE PAINTBRUSH?

The young woman tossed fitfully in her sleep. Things had not been going as she might have wished. First there had been the divorce, then the determination to leave her native Holland and come to Paris to support herself by her painting.

Tonight she had driven herself to the point of exhaustion so that she might collapse into the merciful arms of memory-blotting sleep. But she was too fatigued to sleep restfully. Her mind, prodded into wakefulness by her insistence on working long past midnight, now refused to be stilled, and even though she slept, it was a sleep of the most superficial kind.

"Don't be so lazy, Weisz," she heard a voice say, "get up and work."

Cautiously she opened one eye. There was no one there. She was alone and she knew it.

"Get up, Weisz. Great art is not accomplished while one lies sluggishly in bed."

This time she opened both eyes and propped herself up on an elbow.

"To your easel, Weisz!"

Henriette Weisz-Roos was now wide awake. She was as curious about the voice's insistence in calling her solely by her married name as she was by the eerie fact that there was no body to accompany the voice.

Under her own name, Henriette had acquired a reputation as a Dutch portrait painter. She had married a man named Weisz, whom she had subsequently divorced. Although it is the custom in Holland for divorced women to resume their maiden names, Henriette Roos continued to work under her married name. She was rebuked by her mother for thus flaunting convention, but Henriette explained to her mother that, for some unaccountable reason, she liked the name Weisz.

"It is a very strange feeling," she tried to explain to her perplexed mother, "but somehow that name seems to suit me. I feel one with it. It is more me than my own name, Roos. Whenever people call me by my maiden name, I have the feeling that they are talking to someone else."

At last Henriette decided to compromise with custom and began to call herself Mrs. Weisz-Roos.

But here she was alone in her studio in Paris, with

some disembodied voice calling her by her married name.

"Weisz," the voice insisted. "Get out of bed and stand to your easel!"

At last Henriette obeyed the demands of her invisible taskmaster and slid her feet out from beneath the covers.

"No lights!" the voice cautioned.

"How am I to paint in the dark?" Henriette wondered aloud.

Then, as she described the incident in a personal communication to Dr. Ian Stevenson, who quoted the episode in his essay, "The Evidence for Survival from Claimed Memories of Former Incarnations," Henriette began to paint with feverish haste. She scarcely knew what she was doing, but after a time she felt better, became drowsy, and returned to bed and to sleep.

When she awakened the next morning, she was amazed to discover that she had painted a beautiful little portrait of a young woman.

Henriette was completely puzzled by the whole affair. Later, when she described the uncanny incident to a friend, her confidante recommended that she take the painting to a psychic sensitive who practiced psychometry, the ability to determine information about an object simply by touching it.

When Mrs. Weisz-Roos brought the painting to the sensitive, the clairvoyant took the frame in his hands and lightly touched the surface of the portrait. In what seemed to be only a matter of a few seconds, the man had gone into a trance.

"Letters," he said in a hoarse whisper. "I see very large golden letters. And a name . . . a name is spelled for me. It is G-O-Y-A . . . Goya, the great Spanish painter.

"He tells me that he was forced to fly from his country because of his enemies. It was you who received him in your home; it was you who offered him your protection in your home in a big southern city in France. He lived with you until the end of his life.

"Goya has remained so thankful for your kindness in that life, that he wishes to guide you. You seldom relax your guard. You make it most difficult for him to repay his debt. That was why he made you paint in the dark, so you could not see what you were doing!"

Goya! Henriette Weisz-Roos was stunned. The spirit of the great Spanish painter had come to her. But why? What did the sensitive mean when he said that she had protected Goya in her home in southern France? She was Dutch with no French blood, and she had certainly never owned an estate in France and was not even born until many years after Goya's death. Could the sensitive have been referring to a past life?

Later that same evening, Henriette Weisz-Roos received an answer to the enigma. While she was at the home of a friend, she noticed that her host owned a copy of the life of Goya. As she flipped through the pages seeking a clue to the mystery, she came upon an account of Leocadia Weisz. . . .

THE MURDERED MAN AND THE TEENAGE GIRL

Fourteen-year-old Maria Talarico and a group of her friends stood on the bridge that spanned the Corace River between Siano and Catanzaro, Italy, and stared down at the battered body of the young man that lay sprawled on the rocks of the riverbank far below. It was February 13, 1936.

"What do you think happened, Maria?" asked one of her schoolgirl companions.

"He was a carouser. A no good!" shouted an old woman from the crowd. She had overheard the girl's question and took advantage of the teenager's attention to deliver an impromptu lecture on the evils of the younger generation. "Take heed from his example," the woman told them sternly, wagging a plump finger under their noses. "That is how wastrels end their lives!"

Maria and her friends left the old harridan to shout her lecture to other hapless teenagers. That night, the girl read in the newspaper about the death of Guiseppe Veraldi, who had been found on the rocks below the Corace River bridge. He had been stripped half-naked and his clothes had been scattered about the riverbank. His left arm had been broken and doubled under his chest. Coroners determined that the young man had also suffered a fractured skull. Police ruled that Guiseppe had thrown himself off the bridge in despair over an unfortunate love affair.

Maria Talarico folded the newspaper and decided not to concern her pretty head with another thought about the unfortunate Guiseppe.

Fate, it seems, had decided differently.

Three years later, on January 5, 1939, Maria and her grandmother were crossing the bridge when the seventeen-year-old girl suddenly dropped to the ground in pain. When she was helped to her feet, she was no longer the shy young schoolgirl. She was the brazen and tough Guiseppe "Pepe" Veraldi!

As Pepe, Maria did not recognize a single member of her family. She kept calling for "Mother," but she did not want Mrs. Talarico, she insisted upon Mrs. Caterina Veraldi.

It is fortunate for the annals of psychic research that a number of responsible doctors were available in the village, and each of them kept extensive records of Maria's most mysterious malady.

"I didn't jump off that bridge," Pepe-Maria stormed at the investigators. "That bridge is over one hundred feet high. Do you take me for a fool? I had been drinking and watching my friends play cards at the Gioso Tavern. I left at midnight with Toto, Damiano, Abele, and Rosario. It was those four cowards who beat me and dragged my dead body down to the rocks!"

At last Mrs. Veraldi decided to come to see the girl who claimed to be her son, Pepe. Pepe-Maria was overjoyed at the sight of her. She pulled up a chair for the woman and lavished affection upon her. "Three years!" the girl shouted as "Pepe". "It has been three years since I have seen you."

Mrs. Veraldi had not come without a test for the girl. A brother-in-law unwrapped a picture of Pepe's sister, whom Maria Talarico could never have seen. "Who is this girl, Pepe?" Mrs. Veraldi asked.

Maria-Pepe immediately identified "his" sister and related a humorous incident involving the girl.

"You must not think that I would commit suicide," Pepe's personality beseeched his mother through the person of Maria. "I had been drinking. Twenty-four glasses of wine I had drunk that night. And they put something in my wine. There were four of them. I defended myself as best I could. They beat me with iron bars and stones. They broke my jaw and my arm.

"It is as I have already told the silly police. Did they think that I would jump over one hundred feet and then get up and take off half my clothes? My false friends killed me and dragged me down to the rocks. They took off my clothes and scattered them."

Pepe told his mother and the assembled investigators that one of his murderers, Abele, had died of a heart attack in September of 1938. Toto, according to Pepe, was badly wounded while fighting with Mussolini's army in East Africa. Both statements were later verified as correct.

"The cur, Damiano, is on his way to this house at this very moment," Pepe told the physicians. "He has come to make sport of the little girl who thinks she is Pepe, but I am ready for him!"

Within minutes, Damiano, one of those whom the spirit of Pepe had accused of murdering him, did indeed appear at the door. He barged into the house and immediately charged that those assembled there were as insane as the girl if they believed any of the lies that she had been spreading about him.

Then Pepe began his barrage of questions about the night of the murder. Soon a heavily perspiring Damiano was fleeing from the house. He pushed his way past the physicians, who demanded to question him further, and shouted that he wanted no part of such traffic with the dead.

During Pepe's possession of Maria, the girl was able to recognize all of the murdered young man's friends and relatives and to recall intimate details about each of them. Pepe's memory of his last night alive was vivid, and he named everyone whom he had seen in and about the tavern. Some citizens found themselves embarrassed as Pepe-Maria recalled lovers' liasons that he had observed.

Pepe returned Maria to her rightful inhabitation of her body in as bizarre a manner as he had possessed her. He led the investigators down to the rocks beside the river, stripped off half the girl's clothes, then stretched out the form of Maria Talarico in precisely the same position as Guiseppe Veraldi's body had been found.

The girl lay on the rocks for about ten minutes before she seemingly regained consciousness and began to sit up. One of the men who had followed "Pepe" to the riverbank had covered her nakedness with a coat, but the teenage girl was shocked to find herself in such a state of undress.

Maria had not been left with one shred of memory of the two weeks during which Pepe had possessed her. Shamed by the allegation that she had spent a fortnight claiming to be a man, Maria Talarico went into seclusion and refused to leave her house.

Later, at the request of one of the physicians who had been attending her, Maria issued a statement in which she said she could remember nothing of what others were telling her had transpired during that two week period. She had never dreamed of Guiseppe Veraldi. She had never talked to him while he had been alive. She had never known him or his family. Maria affirmed the fact that she was a healthy seventeen-year-old and had never been ill.

Fortunately, Maria Talarico was in no way mentally impaired by her experience, but she never permitted any of her friends to discuss the incredible two weeks when her body was possessed by the memory patterns of a discarnate personality.

CAN WE REMEMBER OUR ANCESTORS' LIVES?

Can memory be inherited by genetic transmission? The birth of redhead in a family of brunettes is always the subject for a great deal of rather earthy speculation, until it is discovered that great-great-grandfather proudly wore a fiery mane and beard. The unexpected appearance of musical talent in a family of folks "who can't carry a tune in a bucket" or a drunkard in a family of teetotalers may be due to memory-energy patterns transmitted in the genes.

If the miracle of conception, with its pairing of the mother-genes and the father-genes, determine the color of our hair and our eyes, our basic height and weight, our inherent strengths and weaknesses, is it not possible, many researchers are asking, that certain dramatic memory patterns may also be inherited?

In another of my books, I relate the story of how a young Jew in Ireland was "cured" of a crippled hand by the teamwork of a psychiatrist and a psychic sensitive. The sensitive determined that the young man's subconscious carried the violent memories of a Pogrom in Czarist Russia. This particular persecution had included the rape of the young man's female ancestor and the chopping off of the hand of a male ancestor, who had struck back at his attackers.

When the young man was told of the sensitive's impressions of the origin of his physical debility, he remarked to the doctor that it was as if he had heard it all before long ago. Once the seat of the trauma had been discovered, its therapy could be prescribed along the lines of conventional psychoanalysis.

In his article "A Genetic Theory of Reincarnation", which appeared in Fate, Volney G. Mathison wrote that the precise knowledge of "how" we inherit physical and psychical characteristics remains a mystery to science. Some of the genes which we have by chance inherited may have last appeared in a remote ancestor. Incredible as it may seem, only 20 generations back, we each have 1,048,576 ancestors. Only 40 generations back crowds the family tree with over 140 trillion ancestors. On cellular and bioelectronic levels, elements of all of these ancestors are within us, and vast amounts of data are carried in the minute storage area of the electrons.

Mathison theorizes that since our electronic patterns transmit detailed information about our forebears' physical structures, these patterns may also carry memory data relating, he says, to enforced genetic modifications of structure occurring as a consequence of lack of food, injuries in combat, pestilences, and other disasters.

Mathison believes that certain repetitive dreams or hypnotically induced recollections of past lives may be the reactivated expressions of harmful events suffered by some remote ancestor whose genes were inherited.

Obviously, not everyone walks around bent under with the sorrows of the trials and tribulations of his ancestors. What Mathison is postulating is that some individuals may experience disturbing present-moment situations which contain elements *similar* to the disastrous ancient events in their genetic line.

These, he suggests, trigger images, either symbolic or actual, of those ancient, unknown past events which had decisive effects upon one or more of our forebears, and hence, inevitably upon us.

Perhaps such a theory of genetic memory explains the case of a man whom an analyst would refer to only as Harold.

Harold was of Scandinavian stock, and he worked a farm in the heart of rich Midwestern crop land. Since early childhood, Harold had had a morbid fear of fire. This phobia had reached such dramatic proportions that the child would run screaming from the room if a guest lit a cigarette.

Harold's crisis situation was reached when, as a young man of 32, the barn on the family farm caught fire.

Harold's 65-year-old father went into the flaming building in an attempt to lead a prize bull to safety. Timbers collapsed and both Harold's father and the animal were trapped in the flames.

As much as Harold wanted to go to his father's rescue, the young farmer was unable to move from the spot where he lay sobbing and vomitting upon the ground. Fortunately, neighbors arrived in time to rescue Harold's father. The bull had to be destroyed.

The analyst was perplexed because he could find no precipitating trauma in Harold's childhood which would account for his pyrophobia. According to his parents, Harold had "just been born afraid of fire."

This case does not end with a session of hypnotic regression probing the source of Harold's phobia. This particular analyst is much too conservative to employ such "far-fetched" (and time-saving) techniques.

No, in this case it was the patient who provided the key to his problem. Or maybe that is what happens in any successful psychotherapy. At any rate, during one session, Harold brought with him an old leather-bound diary.

"It belonged to my great-grandmother on my mother's side," Harold told the analyst. "It is her journal of the trip across the ocean and her early days on the prairie."

Harold's family maintained close ties with relatives in the "old country," and Harold's parents were able to read Norwegian. The night before, the young man explained, his mother had had an unusual idea and had read aloud a certain section of the journal.

"My great-grandmother writes of a terrible thing that happened to my great-grandfather on the ship coming over," Harold said. "A fire broke out in the ship's galley, and a can of cooking grease exploded.

"Great-grandfather was seated near the galley door at the time, and some of the flaming grease landed on his chest, shoulders, and neck. He received very bad burns, and he nearly died before they reached America. Mother says that he bore the scars from those burns until the day he passed away."

The analyst slowly tapped the point of a pen on his note pad. "And you think there may be some connection between your great-grandfather's severe burns and your fear of fire?"

"Well," Harold said, "you know it's a funny thing, but ever since I was a kid, whenever I would think of fire, I would get a picture of the sea. I could never make any association before. You know, fire and water, complete opposites.

"Then, last night, when Mom was reading from that old diary, I had this funny feeling. I could see it all as she read it, just like I was watching it all on television."

Had the memory, and thereby the fear, of fire been transmitted through the genes from Harold's great-grandfather to his own memory bank?

Volney G. Mathison relates a strangely similar case of a fear of fire that had seemingly been transferred to a descendant by genetic memory.

Connie, a Mexican girl who was employed in Mathison's electronic plant, had been doing a clumsy job of soldering joints and wires. Apparently unaware of her shoddy workmanship, she became extremely upset and irrational whenever she was reprimanded by her supervisor.

Mathison knew that previous analysis had indicated that Connie had "an intense, subconscious terror of getting burned." According to conventional psychoanalytic theory, this meant that Connie had suffered severe burns in childhood or infancy. But she never had, as far as anyone could determine.

Mathison decided, rather reluctantly, to hypnotize Connie and try for a Bridey Murphy type of past-life regression.

While under hypnosis, the girl told of being enroute to the New World on a Spanish sailing vessel! A fire broke out on the crowded 17th century ship, and in the resulting panic, she had been badly burned.

When Mathison brought the girl back to the present, she exclaimed, "Why should I be so afraid of a little old soldering iron after I went through all that?"

It is interesting to note that the girl had a reddish birthmark that covered her back and her right shoulder. According to Mathison, this mark began to diminish in size after the catharsis of the hypnotic session.

A case which seems to be an instance of genetic memory becoming an obsession came to my attention a few years ago. It would seem to fit into our discussion in this chapter, although I will readily concede that the case might also be representative of possession or, perhaps, an instance of extreme ancestor identification.

When Karl Woodstock married Joan, he decided that the perfect place to spend their honeymoon would be his grandfather's old hunting lodge in Northern Michigan. Karl's parents tried to dissuade him from using the old place. No one had used it in years, they argued, and it had fallen into a state of disrepair.

Karl's father had never cared for hunting or fishing and had not been to the cabin since his own father's death, when Karl was 10 years old.

"I got enough of hunting and fishing and getting up at dawn every morning when I was a kid," he would say whenever Karl would beg to go north to the cabin. "I just got sick of it. Besides, spending a day with a fishing pole is like throwing a day away. You can never regain time wasted, boy."

Karl's grandfather had been a professional portrait painter of some repute, and the hunting lodge had been both his retreat and his favorite studio.

"Where better to work than amongst Nature," Karl could remember his grandfather saying. "If my clients can't wait for me to get back to the city, they can come out here to have their portraits painted."

With Grandpa Woodstock, a vacation at the lodge was strictly a busman's holiday. He would rise at dawn for several hours of hunting or fishing, then he would spend the rest of the day at his easel, just as if he were in his studio in the city. The lodge walls were hung with portraits of the Indians, fishermen, hunters, trappers, and dairy farmers who were local residents of the area. These portraits were never for sale, although, on occasion, Karl had known Grandpa Woodstock to give one away to the subject who had patiently sat for him.

Karl's bride, Joan, was a game girl, who did an excellent job of convincing her husband that she would like nothing better than to spend her honeymoon reconditioning a hunting lodge in the north woods. Before their two weeks had ended, however, Joan Woodstock had come to regret the fact that she had not held out for the more conventional Bermuda or Niagara Falls.

On the first night in which they occupied the cabin, Karl found an old family album. The newlyweds were amusing themselves with the snapshots of the child Karl, when the young husband noted a photo of his grandfather with a luxuriant Van Dyke.

"I never knew Grandpa to wear a beard," Karl said. Then, reading the scrawled caption beneath the snapshot, he exclaimed, "No wonder. This was taken thirty years before I was born."

Karl rubbed his chin reflectively, then turned his attention to a number of notebooks which his grandfather had kept during his years of study in Paris. When Joan fell asleep that night, Karl was still reading the journals by the light of a blazing fire.

The new bride woke up alone that morning, a condition to which she would soon become accustomed. She found Karl at the end of the dock. He had risen early to go fishing.

That afternoon, Joan rubbed her cheek after a kiss, and asked Karl if he weren't going to shave. Karl grinned, replied that he had always wanted to grow a beard. Joan rolled eyes heavenward. A honeymoon seemed like a most unlikely time to begin to grow a beard.

When they went into the nearest town for some food supplies that evening, Karl disappeared from Joan's side for a few moments and returned bearing a sack of artist's supplies.

"I was glad that hobby shop had some oils and brushes," Karl said. "The tubes in the cabin have dried out."

"I didn't know you painted," Joan said. "Have you any other hidden talents?"

At the end of the two-week period respectfully set aside as the newlyweds' honeymoon, Karl's parents decided to drive up to the cabin and pay the young couple a surprise visit. The surprise, as it turned out, was on them.

Karl's father was shocked to see his bearded and besmocked son standing before an easel, while the long-suffering Joan sat in a swimming suit, posing for him. Scattered around the studio were a number of portraits in varying stages of completion.

The style in which the paintings were done, according to Karl's father, was that of his own father's early period. Karl's mother later testified to the fact that her son had not previously shown any desire to paint nor had he displayed any creative inclinations. Regarding Karl's physical appearance as he stood behind the easel with his rapidly sprouting Van Dyke, both parents remarked that they felt as if they were seeing a ghost of the boy's grandfather when they first entered the studio.

"Karl looks as Father did when he was young," the senior Woodstock stated. "He resembles Father as he was long before Karl was born."

Karl continued to paint after the young couple had set up housekeeping in their own apartment back in the city. As time passed, however, his painting became progressively worse, and Karl soon lost interest in the easel. Shortly thereafter he had abandoned his oils and brushes, and awoke one morning aghast at what he saw in the bathroom mirror. He immediately set about shaving off his beard.

This case, admittedly, contains a variety of factors which may have brought about Karl's temporary obsession. On the most simple level, we might conclude that Karl suddenly became interested in emulating his grandfather after spending a night reading his journals. This would not, however, account for the considerable talent which the young man originally displayed. A desire to imitate will not substitute for talent no matter how fierce the wish.

Reincarnation *per se* seems out of the question in Karl's case. Karl was a boy of ten when his grandfather passed away. Such a thing as temporary possession by the spirit of his grandfather could remain as a possible hypothesis.

On yet another hand, might not our theory of genetic transmission of memory be considered a very likely explanation? A memory of style, skill, and even appearance transmitted through the genes—a memory that became intensified and stimulated by the young man's moving into an environment in which those memories would have been developed by the original percipients, Karl's father and grandfather.

Because sex is one of man's most basic and powerful drives and because sex is Nature's way of insuring mankind's physical immortality, Volney Mathison has discovered a number of cases in which a violent sexual experience has left a memory pattern that results in problems for future generations.

Mathison relates the case of a married woman whose every contact with her husband would produce in her a severe genital inflammation. This condition was extremely painful and would persist for days after sexual intercourse.

While in deep hypnotic trance, the woman told of a past life in which she had been raped repeatedly by a band of sea coast marauders. The terrible experience left her ancestor with painful injuries.

Mathison states that on the basis of this genetic dream, he "proceeded precisely as in the case of any severe present-life trauma or injurious situation."

In another of the hypnotist's cases, a woefully unattractive spinster was sent to him because she suffered from depression.

While under hypnosis, Mathison says, the woman told of being a beautiful, immoral, and ruthless courtesan who had ruined homes, driven men to duels, and inspired murders.

"I'm 65 and I'm still a virgin," the woman wailed to the hypnotist when they spoke of her present life. "No man has ever wanted to marry me, or wanted me at all . . . no man ever will. I'm the world's ugliest woman. This is my Karma. I'm paying for what I did in previous lifetimes."

Although Dr. Ian Stevenson admits that we have not discovered the limits of genetic transmission, he argues in his essay, "The Evidence for Survival from Claimed Memories of Former Incarnations," that the extension of such a hypothesis to account for the apparent memories of former incarnations meets with serious obstacles.

Dr. Stevenson concedes that genetic memory might apply in instances where the percipient (Person A) belongs to a line descending from Person B, but he points out that in most cases suggestive of reincarnation, the second person was born in another family and in another town. Dr. Stevenson also states that the second birth usually occurred within a few years of the death of the first person. This would make impossible any transmission of information from the first to the second person along genetic lines.

In this view, then, genetic memory may indeed be a possibility, but it has nothing to do with reincarnation. Unless, of course, one were to argue for a Jungian "collective unconscious," in which lie all memories, attitudes, and inclinations that have been amassed by the past of the human race, a collective unconscious into which the transcendent level of every human mind may dip and draw from according to individual need, desire, or longing.

Such a view certainly leaves a physical interpretation of reincarnation for a metaphysical explanation, and we shall take up the matter of "records" of each life on the "Divine Mind" or "cosmic consciousness" in the next chapter.

PAUL TWITCHELL—THIS GENERATION'S EDGAR CAYCE

Certainly one of the most colorful individuals with whom I have traveled into the far reaches of the Unknown is Paul Twitchell, a man who is reputed to be a member of a secret world brotherhood of adepts who use the ancient science of soul travel termed Eckankar to read "Akashic records."

Even the casual reader of psychic adventures will sooner or later find himself confronted by some sort of metaphysics. Metaphysics is much more difficult reading than a collection of weird and unexplainable happenings, and most readers, frightened away by what sounds to them like a curious mixture of philosophy and theology, do not penetrate very far beyond its boundaries. The wisdom and teachings of the East have greatly influenced the metaphysicians and, in turn, those who ponder their writings. Briefly, the Akashic records are said to be the spiritual impressions which each life has made on Divine Consciousness.

The Great Akasha has a record of the divine laws of debt (Karma) and duty (Dharma). Just as the Christian Bible states ". . . whatsoever a man soweth, that shall he also reap," so, insist the adept, do the psychic forces which emanate from us always come full circle and return to us.

In our examination of the various doctrines of reincarnation, we should have to consider ourselves quite remiss if we were to overlook those who claim to read the records set down in the Great Akasha. For a great many people, both in the East and in the West, such readings fully explain the enigma of reincarnation and make of this mystery a very natural aspect of each individual's complete life cycle.

The life readings which were given by Edgar Cayce, the remarkable psychic of Virginia Beach, have received a great deal of publicity and have been quoted in a variety of published forms. Although Cayce has not been with us for a good many years, the impact of the man's work seems steadily to be acquiring new implications for modern man. Intrigued by the very notion of "life readings" and "Akashic records," I brought my questions to Paul Twitchell, a man who may one day be called this generation's Edgar Cayce.

I first made Paul's acquaintance when I was compiling a collection of articles on strange and unusual people and happenings. Paul is the only known Occidental teaching the ancient science of controlled bilocation. In other words, Paul Twitchell can be in two places at once.

Twitchell's friends like to tell of the time when Paul was imprisoned in a South American jail because of a misunderstanding about his passport. To amuse himself and to confound his jailers, Twitchell appeared walking about in a downtown square while his physical body lay on a bunk in the jail cell.

Paul Twitchell is very serious about the applications of controlled bilocation, and with perhaps this one exception, he has never used his ability to project his astral body as a means whereby he might perpetrate a joke. Twitchell uses his unique talent of getting in and out of the body to heal others, even at a distance, to predict the future, and, of course, to read the Akashic records. Twitchell terms this science of soul travel, Eckankar.

"Eckankar is not a philosophy, occult system, religion, or a metaphysical theory," he told me. "It is only a path to God. Just one of many paths, but the one which I know best, since I have used it since childhood."

Paul Twitchell was only five years old when, during a near-fatal bout with pleurisy, his stepsister healed him via astral projection. She slipped into his room late on that night which very likely would have been his last. She sat down beside the bed in a lotus position, took a couple of deep breaths, and slipped out of her physical body into the Atma Sarup, the soul body.

"She took me out with her," Paul recalls, "also in the soul body, and we hung off the ceiling like a pair of eyes viewing the body on the bed below. My stepsister accomplished the healing by impressing the thought that I would be made whole again, upon both my astral and my physical body."

Once Paul knew that all was well and that the living clay lying below them on the bed would once again be his temple, he expressed a reluctance to re-enter the body. He resisted for just a moment, then his stepsister impressed upon him the necessity of returning.

The next moment Paul remembered awakening to find his stepmother and the rest of the family standing by the bed, completely amazed at the swift recovery of their youngest child.

"Two weeks later," Paul says, "when my father returned from overseas, I heard him thank my stepsister for saving my life; it seemed that he had projected himself to the house, from overseas, for the same reason, only to find her taking care of things."

Eckankar Yoga has gained a wide following in the intellectual and college circles of Western Europe, and each spring and summer, Paul Twitchell embarks on a European lecture tour. A number of Twitchell's works have been published in European journals, and his work has been discussed by leading European parapsychologists and psychic researchers.

"The philosophy of Eckankar is that we have proof of survival after death," Paul says. "This is something that many people do not believe, especially the Existentialist crowd. The true purpose of Eckankar is to offer a path to God by offering total awareness via soul travel."

A great deal of this "total awareness," Twitchell believes, comes from a knowledge of one's past lives.

"A good reader of the Akashic records will give his client the events of certain past lives which are affecting him today in this life. It depends upon the judgment of the Akashic reader to give what lives and what events he thinks are causing the present problems and to offer suggestions on how to resolve them."

Paul Twitchell pointed out that too many people want to hear readings which will help to build their own prestige. "They want me to tell them that they have been a queen or some important person in history.

"This is a case of self-defeat, for a reading on past incarnations should be a therapy, a cleansing and understanding of one's past lives. If it isn't, then it does not do one much good."

Twitchell then related the incident of his reading the Akashic records of a middle-aged bachelor.

"He interrupted me and demanded that I give him a vivid account of his sexual adventures in his past lives. I naturally declined."

Through an examination of the Akashic records, Twitchell learned that the bachelor was attached to his mother's apron strings. She controlled the estate which the man would one day inherit, and to please her own selfish whims, she would not permit him to marry.

"This all proved out in his past lives," Twitchell recalls. "There had been a time when he had controlled her in a similar manner and now he was paying for his prior selfishness."

Often a client may have a residual scrap of memory of a former life which influences him to act strangely in his present life. Twitchell mentioned a female client who, as a child, would not allow anyone to call her by any name other than Sally, which was not her name at all.

"Sally was the name of an aunt, who died just before the child was born. The aunt's death was doubly tragic, for not only did she die a very young woman, but she died only a few days before she was to have been married.

"The child grew up with all the characteristics of her aunt Sally. She seemed obsessed with the idea of getting married. Finally, at eighteen, she was wed to a responsible man, who in turn, seemed to have similar characteristics to the man whom her aunt Sally would have married. I suppose she might even have married her aunt's fiance if the man had not met with a fatal accident shortly after the death of the original Sally."

To read the Akashic records, Twitchell must project himself via the atma sarup (soul body) so that he can rise above the time track and read the lives of whomever has requested a reading.

"It doesn't make any difference where the person might be," Twitchell points out. "My client may be in Australia or the Arctic Circle, but, sitting here, I can read his past lives. Once I rise above the time track, the lives of that individual being read are spread out like a fan of playing cards. I must look at the millions of these little file cards, which are memories of the past lives, and select what I believe to be important to my client and the problems which he is facing today. Next, it is up to me to make suggestions as to how he might go about dissolving the Karma (debt) which he has accumulated in a past life.

"Often I have to even go into the lives which a client has spent on the other planes before I am able to return to the physical again. This is not at all hard when one has learned Eckankar, the science of soul travel."

To handle his vast flow of mail, Paul Twitchell maintains a headquarters and staff in Las Vegas, Nevada. Although he is immediately responsive through the mails, Twitchell prefers to remain somewhat aloof to personal contact and to avoid situations which might become psychically depleting. He often refuses to talk with anyone even by telephone. Twitchell does, however, make himself available for public lectures both in this country and abroad, and occasionally conducts workshops in controlled bilocation.

In order to facilitate my research into the enigma of reincarnation, Paul Twitchell granted a request which, frankly, I did not expect. He agreed to open his files to me so that I might make use of any cases which appeared interesting to me and which bore some type of substantiation or response from a satisfied client. Although it is to be hoped that I have gained a reputation for objective reporting, Twitchell's complete compliance to my request certainly demonstrates his sincerity and his confidence.

In the following cases, which have been excerpted from the files of Paul Twitchell, the reader is once again reminded that the author of this book is neither endorsing nor criticizing the metaphysics involved in the reading of "Akashic records." I am simply reporting yet another intriguing facet of the mystery of reincarnation.

When a Mr. B. J. of Nashville, Tennessee wrote to Paul Twitchell for a reading of his personal Akashic records, the practitioner of Eckankar Yoga told him:

". . . At the start of this reading you will be given some of the major incarnations in which your many lives were spent on earth. . . . Each time we take up a new body here on earth, the soul will retain the memory patterns of the lives in the past bodies. But the new brain does not have any memory of these past lives. We have to look into the soul in order to have any recalls of those past lives. Once this happens, our sojourn here is practically over, and we are aware of who we are and what our goal is and we start working to get back into heaven again.

". . . you came into this world about forty thousand years ago, which is not long when compared with many who have been here much longer. But your life has been one of perplexity and fear as to what your mission is in this universe . . . the struggle between the spiritual and the physical natures has caused a lot of disharmony . . . you have far too many sides to your nature for people to understand. . . ."

According to Twitchell, Mr. B. J.'s first incarnation was on the continent of Atlantis, where he was a healer-physician, a wealthy man who chose to work for the poor. Because of his influence with the masses, jealous nobility planted a bit of gossip with the king which convinced him that the healer would eventually turn the masses away from the throne. As a result, the king had his agents assassinate him.

"This was the first karma you had on earth," Twitchell told B. J. "Your first life started out in a series of bloody intrigues that really didn't concern you, but, as usual, the human mind doesn't want anyone to get ahead of himself. These initial intrigues are showing up all through your incarnations here. Soul is always an innocent entity in its life here on earth. It is that part of us which is certainly happy all the time, and if we could revert ourselves back to soul consciousness, then practically all our problems would be dissolved, or at least put under control."

B. J.'s next life was in the land of Egypt under Ramses II, who was the husband of the Queen who found Moses in the river rushes. This time, B. J. was a priest who was very close to the Queen. Acting as the Queen's father confessor, he knew about the young man, who was one of the favorites in the court, but the Pharoah was doubtful that Moses was one of his sons. His suspicions grew stronger when he learned by rumor that Moses was visiting the Jews in Goshen. When Moses persisted in his visits in defiance of the Pharoah's orders to cease venturing to Goshen, he was ordered out of the country. B. J., the priest, defended Moses and wanted to go with the young noble, but he realized that his first duty was to the Queen. Many years later, as an old man, he did follow Moses when he led the Jews out of Egypt. B. J., the priest, died in the wilderness a few months later.

Intrigue continued to cast the pattern of B. J.'s various incarnations, as Twitchell next saw his client as a Roman cavalry officer battling the advancing legions of Hannibal's Carthagians. B. J., the Roman officer, died a violent death in an attempt to kidnap the woman he loved from her family's villa.

Twitchell remarked: "One must remember that these were violent years in the history of the world, and if one was incarnated into this period, it was due to the fact that he was drawn back because of his karmic debt."

Much karmic debt was worked out by B. J. in his next incarnation when he was a priest who spoke out for Jesus during his trial. Declared an outcast for defending a trouble maker, B. J. was condemned to wander until his death.

Twitchell saw a number of more recent incarnations of B. J., but most of the karmic debts that he had accumulated came about during the major lives which we have listed.

"Now the rope is completed in this life," Twitchell told him. "You must work off the debts, in a manner of speaking. This is not the great, difficult task that so many believe. You must put yourself on the path to God . . . then you will start dissolving much of this karma, and all things will start getting better."

Twitchell closed by warning B. J. that he saw a legal matter in the near, if not immediate, future.

In B. J.'s reply to Twitchell's reading, the man remarked: "Paul, I am glad that you mentioned the legal matter that is coming up in the near future . . . I intend to employ an attorney to take care of this matter. It is the leasing of some mineral acreages that I own . . . I have held onto this . . . since I was a boy in the hopes that it would be valuable some day. . . ."

An interesting correspondence was initiated by a Dr. C., who wished to learn if his life had interacted with that of H., his son, in any previous incarnations. The following is excerpted from his files:

"Dear Dr. C.:

"Here are further details on the past lives of your son, which you requested in your letter of March 21st. You will find this reading in greater elaboration than the one sent you January 29th of this year. It will also show more connecting links between you in the past that brought you both together, sometimes in close bond and other times, remotely.

"Since he is an old soul here in this material world, it is only fair to all concerned to show that he had much influence in shaping the lives of those around him for the better. Much of his work, which has been in the field of social justice, certainly changed a lot of customs and traditions in various times as he (his soul) took body after body, down through the centuries. Being a thinker, and one with a purpose, he always came back, intent upon finishing what was started in lives before. Sometimes this was consciously known to him, but many times it was the working of . . . the deep urging of soul to impress his mind to follow the channels of helping others.

"The first of his incarnations in this material universe is found on the planet Jupiter, where he first met with you when you were working in the field of science and religion. You discovered the formula for longevity. He at this time was the minister of civil affairs. He was a very good friend of yours and worked with you closely because of his interest in health of the nation's people.

You both had a very close religious tie, and you were both interested in the worship of one God. The subject of space travel and flying machines used by the Jupiterians was of much interest to both of you. Twice, H. had to appear before the Emperor to defend you on the subject of your work and discoveries.

"Your formula for longevity was stolen by enemy agents and you were accused of selling it to the Sukshams from the planet Mars. H. came to your rescue and saved you from the King's wrath. The formula was recovered before any damage was done, and finally, it was actually lost. But by now the King had accepted you as trustworthy, and he forgot the formula, as long as he was sure it wasn't in enemy hands.

"Next, H. is found again in embodiment on the planet of Venus, a few years prior to your arrival there, for you had stopped on the planet Clarion, where you were doing work in spiritual healing. This time he is a priest in the worship of the mysteries of Dionysius, which later came down to Earth and was established in Greece, as one of the early mystic teachings of the ancient world.

"H. became involved in the continued wars against the raiders from Mars and other warlike planets, when the good King Coth, ruler of Clarion under the Council of Ten, got himself into trouble by declaring a war without permission. He had sought out H.'s advice about the continued raids that were making deep inroads on the planet's business and commerce. But he misunderstood what H. had told him; what H. actually said was that if war was to come, then it would be best to get the planet prepared first. But the King got the idea that war should be declared on any planets where the raids initiated.

"This brought about trouble for H., for when the King faced the Council and said it was H.'s advice, there was little H. could say to correct this impression. As result, H. was ordered to go into seclusion and not to appear again until released from this order. He died in a monastery, not far from the Temple of Dionysius.

"H. bypassed Venus where you stayed for a long time as Haramchis, the High Priest of the Order of Golden Dawn, and went on to Tertan, the ancestrial city of Brest. Briefly, he served as Chief Minister under a sinister dictator, who blocked all social justice that H. tried to bring to the people. He died, but he came back again, this time to the land of Mu, that great continent which filled most of the Pacific Ocean area. Here he was a member of the Holy Brothers in the world which was almost flat as a table top. This was the world before the coming of the magnetic cataclysm, which according to ancient records, brought the waves of seas flooding the earth.

"These Holy Brothers were a group of enlightened men, who went across the world preaching and teaching the light of God. They gave the prophecy that, unless the people would change, very few of them would survive the coming tragedy. H. led his little band through Mexico, part of America, across to Europe, and into Africa and some of Asia. It was the ancient world in those days, but much of civilization was greater than it is now.

"These brothers were later taken into the Order of Golden Dawn, and your paths crossed on Lemuria, where you disguised yourself as a farmer but were actually the leader of the Golden Dawn Order. You were distant cousins at this time. Actually, the two of you were fighting the black magic forces of the Black Brotherhood. But, here in this life, H. died, in the central area of Brazil, knowing that he had completely failed at giving his message to the peoples of the lands where he had traveled.

"Next H. appeared again right after the terrible disaster had struck the world. Now he had to be content with helping to rebuild the new world. The old Aryan empire of Uighur in central Asia was practically destroyed and only a few survivors wandered, destitute, around what is now the Gobi desert. H. pulled them together and showed them how to garden vegetables, build shelters, clothe themselves against climatic conditions, and hunt for whatever game was left. He practically pulled the Aryan race back into existence again, and centuries later, it invaded Northwest India where it settled to become the ruling race for generations.

"H. then went west, working with whatever survivors could be found on the new crust of Earth. He was very successful, and a new world was formed where the old one had been. After doing his work here, H. decided that it was time to return to the Astral plane and wait for a little while before assuming a physical body in reality. H. disappeared for two or more centuries, according to our time here.

"H. reappeared in body form again, in early Egypt under Ramses II. At the same time, you were an engineer for public works in that country. You were interested in Moses, and were killed in a secret meeting when you were attacked by the King's agents.

"At this time, H. made his appearance as a reader for the court. Since few people (including the Pharoah) had the knowledge of reading, someone who was adapted to this art was hired permanently to read the news and other official communications sent to the court. Most communication was verbal, but not trusting his couriers, Ramses II made his agents in the field send news by tablets and papyrus.

"It was through you that H. became interested in Moses and involved in helping the Israelites to be freed of their bondage. H. finally left the court and started giving full time to the cause. When the Israelites were able to leave the country, H. accompanied them, but he died in the wilderness.

"H. went through several other incarnations in the Middle East: in Uruk, in Babylon, in the old city of Damagg, in China under Shang dynasty, as a mystic in Central China, and as a warrior at the city of Mohenjo-Daro, in the Valley of Indus of early India.

"Another important incarnation was in ancient Greece. This time he was a King at Attica, and he was known as a great one, because of his liberal views in helping the common people. His upper class fought him bitterly over this, for it meant the weakening of their hold on political and economic matters. This was the cause of the downfall of his city-nation, for one night some of the masses opened the gates of the city to the enemy and all was lost. H. was killed in the attack.

"H. reincarnated in Crete as a bull dancer. Again in Greece, as a prophet who forecast the outcome of Phillip of Macedon's campaigns. Then H. got back into body as a mystic and preacher in ancient China. During these periods, H. found a relationship with you in many capacities, as described in other readings sent to you over the past few months.

"During the early years of Rome, when Rome and Carthage were at war, H. lived in Rome as an official artist for the Republic. When Scipio was commanding the Roman legions in Spain and later against Carthage, H. was sent to North Africa with the legions to record the campaign by pictures. He was at Utica when he saw a young, lovely Carthaginian slave-woman with whom he fell in love. H. went to Scipio, under whose direct command he was serving, and asked for her.

Scipio was amused and curious at the request, for he, as a Roman, believed that it was beneath the dignity of anyone to ask for a slave as a wife. Nobody in Rome fell in love with a slave; they were for amusement only.

"When Scipio saw the woman, he was so struck by her beauty that he took her for himself. H. became unhappy over this, and he tried to rescue the woman, in the hope that they could escape into the desert. But H. was killed by a guard before they could get away. This woman is the feminine soul that will later come into H.'s life during his adult years and reclaim her love for him. It will be a mutual happiness.

H. was in Palestine during the time of Christ's ministry, where he was a legal counselor for Pontius Pilate, then the Provincial Governor for the Roman rule over Palestine.

"When Christ was brought before Pilate, the governor asked H.'s advice on the legal aspects of the trial. H. pointed out that Pilate had no legal hold on this man, nor did the priests, and advised Pilate not to have anything to do with the situation. But Pilate disregarded the advice, turned Christ over to the Temple council, and let them proceed with the trial. H. was very impressed with Christ at the time, but died before following out any ideas on the new sect.

"Then H. went through a number of other incarnations: in Greece as a priest at the Oracle of Delphi; a soldier under Clovis; lawyer during Justin II's reign and others where your paths crossed many times over.

"H. is found again at the signing of the Magna Charta. Following this life, he came back in England as a friend of Edward III, who was responsible for the English law which gave the common man a chance to defend himself in court. H. was in several Crusades. He served in Sweden for a life under Charles XII, as a military chief. In another incarnation, H. defended the policy of Savonarola, the monk who sought to reform the Church.

"There are many incarnations that H. went through during his past journey down through the centuries. These are fitted in where many of his other incarnations have been explained in a previous reading. Following his incarnation in the Napoleonic wars as a gunner, he came back again as a friend of George Sand, Chopin, and some of the greats in the last century. In fact, he was in love with George Sand, alias for Aurore Dudevant, the famous woman writer of the 19th century. At the time he was himself a writer, a critic of plays and dramatic subjects for one of the newspapers in Paris. His love never was realized because of her affection for Chopin. He died about 1878, of a fever."

Twitchell gave an intriguing reading for a Mrs. L H. of Mohawk, New York. The adept told Mrs. L. H. that, from her first incarnation, her "pride has been great, but courageous to the point of sometimes losing your life. Yet your temper has been too strong, forceful and unpleasant at times. It has been this quality which has hurt your health so much even in this life. This is one of the threads of karma which has come down into this present time."

As an aside, Twitchell told the woman: "Please don't think that karma is all evil, for it isn't. The word karma is used for the whole law of retribution, or cause and effect. It is a counter check, a balance between the good and the bad of one's conduct and experiences on earth. It keeps the bad from overbalancing the good, and vice versa. As in your case, you are now paying for this karma with your bad health and afflictions. One must either go through these experiences or learn to avoid them. Often a high teacher can dispel karma for one, but on the other hand, he may not because he sees that the *chela* must earn his right to be freed of this karma only by going through it to get the experience. Since it is only experiences which make us aware of the Ultimate Kingdom of God, then it is experiences that purify us and make us eligible to enter into the kingdom again."

Mrs. L. H. was controlled by pride during her first incarnation as a priestess in the Temple of the Bull on Crete. As a male poet under one of the early Shang rulers in China, L. H. stubbornly fought the emperor for peasant reforms. As the wife of a wine merchant in Jerusalem, L. H. became a fanatical follower of Christ. As a monk in old England, L. H. failed to warn Thomas a'Becket of the plot against his life and silently watched the clergyman go to his death.

But the most significant of L. H.'s incarnations was during the persecution of the Christians under Nero when, because she adamantly refused to betray her friends, her eyes were put out with hot irons.

In her letter of response to Twitchell's reading, Mrs. L. H. wrote: "My Akashic record received and read many times with great interest and increased understanding of many things. You are a wonderful man to do such excellent work.

"I was thrilled to learn about my life in the time of Jesus, for I have had vibrations in that respect, but I hardly thought I deserved such an honor. . . .

"I have a question about my eyes . . . You say this is mainly the problem with my eyes today. No doubt you mean the blindness, or do you mean the pain also? During most of this life, I have suffered aching and distress in my eyeballs with frequent spells of very severe pain, like something boring into my eyes, unbearable at times. . . .

"I was very pleased when you said that I was a fine pianist in France . . . I have always had a strong desire for piano music in this life. . . ."

To Mrs. L. H.'s husband, Twitchell wrote: "You have a love which has sustained you for centuries. You should never feel parted because of this love . . . it has wrapped a protective aura around her throughout the centuries, whether you were the husband, friend, wife, relative, or any other person close to her. . . . You have been a good combination with your wife, in this life and in past lives. You and she have been in a varied number of lives, especially the ones that I have named. You were the husband in the last one, the Englishman that she married. Often you were the wife. But you have always been together and that is the most important part about your relationship."

To answer my query concerning the relationship between the dogma of reincarnation and the signs of the Zodiac, Twitchell replied: "This is one of the most important and interesting aspects of reincarnation.

"It is necessary, according to the teachings of Eckankar, to have a birth within each sign of the Zodiac. This is what Buddha described as the Wheel of the Eighty Four. We each go around the Zodiac with rebirth in each sign, many times, and often rebirths one after the other within a sign, until we are put on the path to God or reach God-Illumination.

"Once we have had some degree of this God-Illumination or have entered into the Kingdom of Heaven (words used to describe the ultimate realm of God) then we are without need to reincarnate again. We are on the heavenly path to God and will continue to go up the ladder until reaching the ultimate kingdom.

"What I am saying here is that we do not reincarnate again on the physical plane; but we, as soul, go to the astral plane and live there for a while, then up to the casual or mental plane. Then we will go through the same process between planes of having to be reborn again on the lower plane, maybe the astral, or casual, until we are off that lower plane and into the higher. This process goes on until we are able to reach the fifth state of consciousness where we are established and become liberated from reincarnations on any lower planes.

"This is the whole purpose of Eckankar: to give one liberation during his lifetime. Once a spiritual traveler (master, *guru,* or whatever one wishes to call these higher souls) takes him under instruction, the student is gradually taken to the fifth plane of consciousness, sometimes called the soul plane—the dividing line between the lower worlds and the worlds of pure spirit (God). Once established on this plane, the student becomes free and can travel without the assistance of a master. He can live in this physical body until his days are over on this world and go on to the God-worlds after death without help from anyone, and he does not need to have to undergo the process of reincarnation again."

The following excerpts illustrate another facet of Mr. Twitchell's readings. The request was made by the sister of Mr. E. F., who was ill, and whose sister was quite naturally concerned for him.

"Dear Miss S. F.:

"It is my pleasure to have this opportunity to do this Akashic reading for your brother via soul projection—the separation of spirit from the body—which is the procedure which I use to look at the etheric records of anyone while I am out of the physical body (with their permission, of course).

"Generally, I will not do a reading for anyone when requested by another, but in the case of illness, as you have pointed out, an exception is made. However, to continue, I wish to point out that Mr. F. is surrounded by a deep brown and yellow color, which is, of course, the aura about his spiritual body. It means that he is living in a dualistic world, his physical consciousness is pulled into the materialistic region, while soul is trying to keep a higher state of consciousness, but not exactly doing so. There is a strong pull on his mind to go two ways, splitting it into sections, and frankly keeping him from having any reality on present time.

"This is one of the great troubles in our society, for the psychic forces which pull the individual in many ways splits him into little pieces and he generally ends up in an institution. Too many of our present members of this society cannot recognize the psychic forces at work in an individual. Usually, as in the case of Mr. F. it's a case of a child being too sensitive to the inner powers when there is no one to help him. But I will discuss more of this in the consultation which is to follow this reading.

"The reason we are here instead of heaven is simply that we are sent to the physical planes to gain experience, like a child is sent to school to get his education. Eventually we will, after many incarnations here, gain varied experiences which will purify souls so that we may return to heaven where we will be ready to serve God as a co-worker.

"I am going to bypass the depth of many of Mr. F.'s incarnations to show how his illness has happened and why it is, in his present life, working out as a karmic condition. In this reading we will discuss several of his major incarnations to find out what has happened in the past and put it up to date.

"Mr. F. stepped across the borders of the spirit worlds into the lower universe many centuries ago, in fact so many that it is impossible to determine just when it was, according to the matter of year and date. But it was on the planet of Mercury that he first saw this universe and mingled with the intellectual citizens there." Hereafter follows a detailed analysis of Mr. F.'s "lives," ending with, those named here. "You were mentioned several times where it was a close tie with him, but you and he have been together for a long time, in many lives."

The clients who ask Paul Twitchell for life-readings

seem immensely satisfied with the result which this adept produces. Whether Twitchell actually touches upon certain "memories" which the clients sense or whether he, through some clairvoyant faculty, is able to provide them with readings which suit their temperaments, psychological needs, and secret longings is not within the consideration of this present book. I do know that I read several letters such as this one, from a Mr. H. R. of Overton, Nevada:

"I found the entire reading both intriguing and enlightening . . . after receiving the reading and studying it very thoroughly, I have noted a substantial improvement in my outlook and my ability to maintain a steadier level of emotional stability . . . it (the reading) has been of distinct benefit as well as of interest.

"I especially want to thank you for helping my mother, as she has noted a most remarkable improvement in her general level of health since my last letter to you."

What about Paul Twitchell himself? Does he recall any of his past lives? Is he able to read his own Akashic records?

In the January-February 1967 issue of *Orion* magazine, Twitchell wrote: "During the 6th century B.C., when I studied under the great Pythagoras of Greece, I learned that he was concerned mainly with two points in the teaching of truth. First, emphasis on love, wisdom, and charity, and secondly, that the Kingdom of Heaven was within man.

"This was the basic point of his teachings. It disturbed the priestcraft of his day so much that, after his death in 500 B.C., the masses were incited to attack and destroy Pythagoras' followers and schools at Crotona and Metapontum. Fortunately, I escaped both disasters, including the fate of those who were compelled to die of hunger and thirst in the Temple of the Muses."

When a reader of one of his articles criticized Twitchell's statement that he could trace his own past lives as far back as eight million years ago, Paul sent me the man's letter with a note of his own attached: "It's true. I can trace my lives back this far, but I would never attempt to give anyone a reading on his reincarnations this far back! It would shock a person's senses too badly."

Akashic records, Karma and Dharma, systematic rebirths, all add yet another strand to the powerful rope that binds the enigma of reincarnation.

THE MAN WHO RETURNED AS HIS GRANDSON

Mrs. Susan George was sorting through her jewelry box that afternoon when her son, William, wandered into her bedroom from the room in which he had been playing.

Fascinated by his mother's treasures, the five-year-old boy stood at the side of the bed where she had arranged her earrings, bracelets, necklaces, and pins. Then, spotting the gold watch which she lifted from the jewelry box, he suddenly reached out for the timepiece.

"William!" Mrs. George scolded. "Mustn't touch!"

"But it is mine!" the boy shouted. "That is my gold watch!"

"Shush," Mrs. George scowled. "That watch belonged to your grandfather. The same Grandpa William whose name you bear. He asked your momma to keep the watch for him."

"Yes," insisted William. "And that is *my* watch!"

The boy clung to the watch, and it took his mother several minutes to persuade him to allow her to replace it in the jewelry box. When Mrs. George told her husband, Reginald, about the incident, both of them were puzzled by the boy's behavior.

The Georges are Tlingit Indians who live in southeastern Alaska. Like other Tlingits, the Georges believe in reincarnation. Ever since their son William was born, he had given evidence of resembling his paternal grandfather in birthmarks, attitudes, and physical appearance. Although such things were within the realm of their personal beliefs, the Georges found that a manifestation of the doctrine of reincarnation occurring in their own home was more than a little disconcerting.

In his article, "Cultural Patterns in Cases Suggestive of Reincarnation Among the Tlingit Indians of Southeastern Alaska" (*Journal* A.S.P.R., Vol. 60, July, 1966), Dr. Ian Stevenson analyzes the data of forty-three Tlingit cases. Surely the case of the fisherman who returned as his own grandson must rank as one of the most amazing and one of the most well-documented of contemporary studies of possible reincarnation.

William George I, had been a well-known Alaskan fisherman, a healthy, robust man, who had always been extremely active. As he grew older, the fisherman, in spite of the fact that he, like his fellow Tlingits believed in reincarnation, began to experience certain doubts and uncertainties about the afterlife.

Often, when he and his favorite son, Reginald, were out fishing, the older man would say, "If there is really anything to this business of rebirth, I will come back and be your son."

On a number of occasions, William made such a statement to his daughter-in-law, Susan. Ignoring the laughter of the young people, the fisherman would expand his statement by saying that they would be able to recognize him by the fact that he would be reborn with the same birthmarks as the ones he presently bore. These birthmarks were well-known by his friends and kin to be two large moles, each about half an inch in diameter, one on his upper left shoulder and the other on his left forearm.

William George continued to discuss his plans for a return to life in the form of Reginald's son, and he became increasingly serious about the matter. In the summer of 1949, he gave Reginald his gold watch.

"This was given to me by your mother, as you well know," William told his son. "I want you to take it now, and I want you to keep it for me. When I come back as your son, I'll reclaim the watch, so you take good care of it for me."

Reginald told his father not to dwell on such a morbid subject. The elder George was in fine health, 60 years old, and should be able to look forward to several more productive years. Reginald told his father to keep his watch and to plan to carry it for many years to come.

William George was insistent. "I don't have long, and I don't want any harm to come to the watch. If there is anything to this business of reincarnation, I'll be back as your son and I'll get my watch back then."

Reginald could see that there was no use in arguing further with his determined father. He went home for the weekend, told his wife what his father had said.

"You might as well go along with him," Susan George advised her husband. "I'll put his watch in my jewelry box. It'll be safe there."

A few weeks later, in August, the crew of William George's seine boat reported their captain as missing. None of them could say what had happened to their skipper. His body was never recovered, and they could only conclude that he had fallen overboard and had been swept away by the tide.

On May 5, 1950, scarcely nine months after William George's death, his daughter-in-law, Susan George, went into labor.

As she lay in the delivery room waiting for the anesthetic that would remove her consciousness, Susan George thought she saw the form of her father-in-law standing at her side. The vision was so real and the actions of the image so life-like that Mrs. George came out of the anesthetic uttering soft cries of confusion. She awoke fully expecting to see an apparition of William George still hovering in her room.

Mrs. George saw no apparition, but she was presented with a healthy baby, a boy who had a large mole on his left shoulder and another on his left forearm. Both birthmarks were in precisely the same location as those borne by his grandfather.

Reginald and Susan George were confused. It seemed as though William George had returned just as he had promised. At any rate, the couple felt that the exact placement of the moles justified their naming their son, William George, II.

As the boy began to grow up, his parents found an ever-increasing number of details which tended to justify their decision to name their son after his grandfather. The boy's behavior traits, his likes, dislikes, and skills coincided exactly with those of William George I.

Foremost among the many similarities was the peculiar manner in which the boy walked. His grandfather, when a young man, had injured his right ankle severely while playing basketball. William George, Sr. had walked with a limp for as long as most members of the fishing village could remember. Because of the nature of the injury, William had turned his right foot outward so that he walked with a peculiar gait which became a characteristic of the man. Reginald and Susan George were startled when their young son took his first steps with his right foot turned outward. In spite of their efforts to guide the boy into a proper gait, he persisted in maintaining the peculiar, twisted manner of walking.

"He is the image of his grandfather," members of the George family have told investigators. "Not only does he look like him, he worries like him."

The Alaskan fisherman, for all his bravado and skill aboard his boat, was known as a great worrier. His constantly repeated words of cautionary advice to his crew often brought groans of irritation from seamen who felt that they knew their business at least as well as their captain. William, I also has the habit of giving unsolicited advice to much older and more experienced seamen. When Dr. Stevenson investigated the case in 1961 the boy had gained the reputation of being fretful and overly cautious. It was especially noted that William, II had a morbid fear of the water.

"But he certainly knows his fishing and his boats," one fisherman testified. "The first time he was put in a boat he already knew how to work the nets."

"And he knew all the best bays for fishing and how best to work them," another fisherman put in.

William George, II has always referred to his greataunt as his *sister*. His uncles and aunts (Reginald's brothers and sisters) have always been his "sons" and "daughters." In gruff tones, he has scolded two of his "sons" (uncles) about their excessive use of alcohol. William's own brothers and sisters often call him "grandpa," a title to which he has never objected.

In recent years, William, II has been discouraged from talking about his former life. Older members of the Tlingit village have warned his parents about the dangers of recalling a past life, and Reginald and Susan have heeded this advice.

"His mind had begun to wander," Reginald said. "He

was becoming more concerned about the past than about the present and the future. This can be very harmful."

Although he has ceased to speak in excessive measures about his past life as his grandfather, William, II still persists in asking for "his" gold watch.

"I should have it now that I am older," he maintains.

BACK TO MOTHER'S ARMS

Sleep had been out of the question for Mrs. Carmelo Samona of Palermo, Sicily, ever since her daughter, Alexandrina, had died three days before.

The five-year-old girl had passed away suddenly of meningitis on March 15, 1910, and there had been nothing that even her physician father had been able to do to preserve her life.

Then, on the third night of her grief, Mrs. Samona at last succumbed to a sleep born of exhaustion. It was during that night that she had a dream in which she saw the form of her deceased daughter.

In a soft and comforting voice, Alexandrina told her mother not to weep any more.

"I shall come back to you," Alexandrina said. "I shall be little again, like this." The girl made motions with her arms, as if she were pantomiming the holding of a small baby.

Mrs. Samona told her husband nothing of the first dream, but when she had a repetition of the strange vision three nights later, she related the details to Dr. Samona.

As time passed, Mrs. Samona was given the startling

information that she would soon bear twin girls. One of the girls, according to the spirit of Alexandrina, would be a new life, the other would serve as the vessel whereby she might return to earth.

Dr. Samona reacted with harsh skepticism to the information which his wife relayed to him from her dreams.

Pregnancy seemed out of the question for Mrs. Samona, to say nothing of twins! His wife had undergone an operation after the birth of Alexandrina which would have either greatly reduced her fertility or destroyed it altogether.

Alexandrina's words were prophetic, however, and, within a year, Mrs. Samona gave birth to twin girls.

"See," she told her husband when the nurse brought the babies to her, "see how the one looks exactly like Alexandrina when she was a baby!"

Dr. Samona conceded that there was a strong resemblance, and however he might have truly felt about the matter at the time, he acquiesced to his wife's wish to name the girl Alexandrina II.

As the child matured, Dr. Samona was forced to admit that Alexandrina II bore an increasingly strong resemblance to their deceased daughter, not only in appearance but also in mental attitudes and idiosyncrasies of taste. In addition, both Alexandrinas were left-handed, whereas none of the other Samona children had this trait. Other shared physical debilities included a slight discharge from the right ear, hyperaemia of the left eye, and slight facial asymmetry.

G. Delanne, in his *Documents por Servir a l'Etude de al Reincarnation*, 1924, (quoted in Dr. Ian Stevenson's essay, "The Evidence for Survival from Claimed Memories of Former Incarnations,") conducts an interview with Dr. Samona in which the physician comments:

"I can affirm in the most positive manner that in every

way, except for hair and eyes, which are actually a little lighter than those of the first Alexandrina at the same age, the resemblance continues to be perfect. But even more on the physical side, the psychological similarity developing in the child gives the case in question further and greater interest.

"Alexandrina is indifferent to dolls and prefers to play with children her own age, a preference which was equally noticeable with the other Alexandrina. Like her, too, she is always anxious that her little hands should be clean and insists on having them washed if they are in the least degree dirty.

"Like her predecessor again, she shows a singular repugnance for cheese and will not touch soup if it has the least taste of cheese in it.

"When she has a chance of opening the chest of drawers in the bedroom it is a great amusement to her to pull out the stockings and to play with them. This was also a passion of the other Alexandrina."

Further evidence which seemed to point to Alexandrina's physical return continued to occur throughout her childhood.

When the girl was eight, the Samonas told the twins that the family was planning an outing at Monreale so that they could see the sights there.

Alexandrina II interrupted her mother's enthusiastic recitation with a childish moan of impatience. When Mrs. Samona inquired of her daughter why she seemed apathetic about the coming vacation trip, Alexandrina complained that she knew Monreale and that she had already seen the sights there.

"Surely you are confused with some other city," Mrs. Samona told her daughter. "You have never been to Monreale."

"Yes I have, mother," the girl sighed. "Don't you remember the big church with the statue of the man with his arms held open on the roof?"

"Perhaps you have seen pictures. . . ."

"No, mother," Alexandrina II interrupted. "You can't have forgotten that we went there with a lady who had horns on her head. And don't you remember our meeting some little red priests in the town?"

Upon her daughter's prompting, Mrs. Samona remembered that the last time she had visited the city of Monreale had been nearly ten years before, just a few months prior to Alexandrina I's death. A lady friend of the family had accompanied them to Palermo for medical aid in connection with the removal of disfiguring excrescences on her forehead. She further recollected that they had met a group of young priests dressed in blue robes with red ornamentation as they were entering the church.

The intriguing part of this particular exchange is that Alexandrina II seemed to "remember" *incidents* rather than recite travelogue-type information which she could have acquired from seeing pictures or reading articles about Monreale. Then, too, the incidents recalled were so inconsequential to Mrs. Samona that she remembered them only with great difficulty. It is most unlikely that she would ever have discussed a visit which she considered so unimportant with Alexandrina II at an earlier time. Until prompted by the child, the mother seemed to have forgotten the details of the trip to Monreale which had been made before the death of Alexandrina I

A similar tale of a return to mother's arms is cited in the Honorable Ralph Shirley's *The Problem of Rebirth*

In this instance, Captain and Mrs. Battista of Rome, Italy, lost their little daughter, Blanche. The child had been especially fond of a French lullaby which Marie, her Swiss "Nannie" had taught her to sing. After Blanche death, Marie returned to Switzerland, and because of the painful memories which the strains of the lullaby would cause to return, Captain and Mrs. Battista completely blotted all recollection of the tune from their minds.

Mrs. Battista did not become pregnant again until three years after Blanche had passed away. During the fourth month of her pregnancy, she had a vision in which her deceased daughter appeared to her and said, "Mother, I am coming back."

Captain Battista was skeptical of such a message and tried to convince his wife that she had been dreaming.

Mrs. Battista insisted that she had perceived a vision.

"It was no dream," she argued. "I heard Blanche's sweet and familiar voice tell me that she was going to return to us."

When the baby, a daughter, was born that next February, Captain Battista gave in to his wife's demands that this daughter should also be christened Blanche.

"Such a thing is not right," he protested, but his wife's earnest desire soon quieted his feelings of discomfort.

Then, nine years after the death of Blanche I, when Blanche II was about six years old, a most extraordinary thing occurred.

The Battistas were seated in the study, which adjoined the bedroom where their daughter slept, when they both heard "like a distant echo, the famous cradle song."

They found Blanche II sitting up on her bed, singing the song with a faultless French accent. Neither of the Battistas had taught the song to the child. In fact, they had long ago made a pact never to refer to the lullaby in any way.

"What," Mrs. Battista began hesitantly, "what is that you are singing, Blanche?"

"I am singing a French song," the child answered simply.

"Who taught you such a pretty song?" Captain Battista asked.

"Nobody," shrugged Blanche II. "I just know it out of my own head."

Then, while the Battistas stared at each other in wonder, the child once again sang the lullaby as gaily "as if she had never sung another song in her life."

Captain Battista concludes his story by writing: "The reader may draw any conclusion he likes from this faithful narrative of facts to which I bear my personal witness. For myself, the conclusion I draw from them is that the dead return."

EAST IS EAST AND WEST IS WEST

As we have previously noted in the chapter, "Remembrances of Lives Past," it is not a simple matter to obtain cases suggestive of reincarnation in the United States, or, for that matter, the whole of the Western world. Even though many of the great minds who shaped the intellectual and religious climate of the West held firm beliefs in reincarnation (i.e. Plato, St. Augustine, St. Clement, St. Jerome), historically, at least since the fourth century A.D., the ecclesiastical dogmatists have spoken out against the doctrine of rebirth. Only a slightly more liberal attitude exists today, and American parents would certainly not encourage a kindergartener to come forward with alleged memories of a prior existence. Doctor, priest, and P.T.A. would descend upon the unfortunate child with the fervor of Grand Inquisitors.

Dr. Ian Stevenson, who has done a great deal of investigation into situations wherein individuals have claimed to recall former lives, has amassed more than 600 cases suggestive of reincarnation. The researcher, presently of the Department of Neurology and Psychiatry of the University of Virginia, has found these cases distributed all over the globe, among peoples of widely varying cultural patterns, and among societies where the religious dogmas sternly preach against a belief in reincarnation.

As the reader progresses into his study of this subject, he will note, as did Dr. Stevenson, that cases suggestive of reincarnation all have certain factors in common which seem completely unrelated to and independent of the percipient's cultural environment. Whether the case should occur in India, England, or the United States, certain basic features remain constant:

A small child, two to four years of age, begins to protest to his parents or brothers and sisters that he wishes to return to his former home, wife, children, or possessions. The child graphically describes his former life and generally expresses a dissatisfaction with his inability to return to the geographical environment which he was forced to leave at the event of his death.

A point to be stressed is that, even though the majority of Eastern cultures (Indian, Ceylonese, Burmese) maintain a belief in reincarnation as a part of their religious faiths, young children are definitely not encouraged to "remember" past lives. On the contrary, a child who claims such memories will generally be strongly admonished to forget the whole thing. In the cases which follow, we will see that the parents often felt no compunction in administering physical punishment when their offspring persisted in claiming memories of a prior existence.

In spite of threats of punishment and a chorus of mockery from his siblings, we see that the child persists in his allegations. He experiences a strong pull back toward the life that has recently terminated, and he continues to beg his present parents to allow him to return to the community where he lived in his previous incarnation.

If the child continues in his persistence and in his recall of intimate details of another existence, the parents may reluctantly begin to make inquiries about the accuracy of the story which their child babbles. In many cases, the investigation will not have occurred until several years after the child has begun to speak of his memories. In each of the cases which we shall examine, we shall see that this delay in investigation speaks very convincingly against any charge of conspiracy or fraud on the part of the parents. In many of the stories presented in this book, the parents have reacted with emotions and attitudes ranging from disinterest to violent anger when their child persisted in his claims of a previous incarnation. All of the parents were publicity shy and had no desire to put their offspring on display for monetary gain.

If the parents do begin some attempts at verification and if some positive results are obtained, members of the two families involved may visit each other for the purpose of interrogating the child. He may be asked if he remembers persons, objects, past incidents, and personal experiences of his alleged previous existence. If the child scores an impressive series of hits, his story will create a great deal of attention in the communities involved and, in most cases, local newspapers will be alerted to the event.

In recent years, the Indian Society for Psychical Research has sent investigators to document cases suggestive of reincarnation, but it is impossible to determine how many dramatic cases have never been researched due to angry and frustrated parents suppressing a child's memories with threats and demonstrations of physical punishment. Even though the religions of India may include reincarnation in their doctrines, I feel we must re-emphasize the fact that no Indian mother crouches over her child's cradle at night and encourages him to recall a past life.

I think another most impressive point in the cases which we shall examine is the early age at which the child begins to graphically describe a former life. It would seem to be beyond belief that a two-year-old boy could speak so eloquently in protest of his murder at the hands of a debtor, solely from the aspect of the mechanics of speech and articulation, let alone the manifestation of reincarnation.

In each of the following cases, the young child truly seems to be an "old soul," much advanced beyond his peer group in proficiency of speech, application of intellect, and sociability. Imagine the reaction of the various widows, whom we shall meet in these chapters, when they hear intimate details of their marriage relationship from the lips of two-year-old boys, who continue to speak frankly of matters which only their husbands would know.

Truly, fraud would seem to be out of the question in such cases. No two-year-old is capable of being coached to perpetrate such elaborate hoaxes. No child's brain is capable of memorizing countless details of the lives of obscure men and women who died in remote and desolate villages. And what motive would a parent have to precipitate such a hoax? What would justify the countless hours necessary to coach a two-year-old to recite the details of the life of a housewife of a butcher in a nearby village? The Indian newspapers do not offer a reward for the year's best case suggestive of reincarnation.

No, something is at work here. Whether it be extrasensory perception, possession by a discarnate soul, or reincarnation will be judged according to the personal bias of each reader. All that I shall present are the documented facts.

"DON'T CALL ME ISMAIL!"

The young boy looked at his father, lying on the bed beside him, and said, "I am tired of living here. I want to go back to my house and children."

Mehemet Altinklish listened to these strange notions coming from the mouth of his son Ismail—a mere child of eighteen months! "What did you say, Ismail?" he asked.

"Don't call me Ismail," the boy insisted. "I am Abeit."

Upon being questioned by his father, the boy insisted that he was the reincarnation of Abeit Suzulmus, a prosperous market gardener who had been murdered shortly before Ismail's birth.

Abeit, who lived in the Bahchehe section of the Midik District of Adana, Turkey, had gardens of sufficient size that it was necessary for him to hire laborers. Three such laborers came to him looking for work one day and he employed them. For unknown reasons, they lured Abeit into his stable and there beat him to death with an iron bar.

The killers then went to the house and slaughtered

Abeit's second wife, Sahida, and two of their children. The murders took place on January 31, 1956.

A week later the killers were caught. They were tried and convicted. Two were hanged; the other died in prison.

A few short months after the murders, Ismail was born in another section of the Midik District, about three-quarters of a mile from Abeit's gardens. From the time he was a year and a half old, the boy insisted that he was Abeit Suzulmus, exhibiting a very strong identification with the murdered man. So strong was this identification that he continually begged his parents to let him visit Abeit's home.

When he reached the age of three, his parents finally agreed to such a trip.

Leading a party of twelve, young Ismail traversed the distance between the homes unaided and without error, even though several members of the party deliberately tried to lead him astray. As young as he was and never having wandered very far from his present home, it is highly unlikely that Ismail could have made the complicated journey without some prior knowledge or familiarity with the route. Ismail claimed to have attained this familiarity from his previous life.

When the group reached the house, Ismail identified the members of Abeit's family from a crowd of about thirty persons, calling them by name and embracing them as he did so. He referred to them as Hatice, "my first wife," Gulsarin, "my daughter," Hikmat, "my daughter," and Zaki, "my son."

During this first visit, the boy led the party to the two-room stable saying, "Let me show you where I was murdered," and he pointed to the exact spot. Abeit-Ismail also commented that some of the equipment and furnishings in the stable had been removed since his death.

141

In another revelation of the life of Abeit, Ismail stated that, at one time during his life, Abeit loaned money to Abdul, but they did not know the amount of the loan nor whether it had ever been repaid. Abdul confirmed the fact that he still owed money to the Suzulmus family.

The Adana press carried an incident occurring between Ismail and an ice-cream vendor, who seldom visited the area of Ismail's home. According to the newspaper, Ismail confronted the vendor, a man called Mehemet, and asked if he recognized him. When the vendor replied in the negative, Ismail said, "You have forgotten me. I am Abeit. You did not sell ice cream before, but watermelons and vegetables."

The vendor said that this was true. Ismail went on to tell the vendor about a time when he, Abeit, had performed the circumcision ceremony for him. When they parted, the vendor was thoroughly convinced that he had met Abeit in a new life.

Another time, a cowherd named Mezit, who was employed by the Suzulmus family, was leading a cow past the Altinklish home. Ismail recognized Mezit, calling him by name and inquiring whether the cow was his (Abeit's) "yellow girl."

So real are the memory patterns of Abeit to Ismail that he often speaks of his former life in the present tense, such as, "I have a house and family," or "Here is my grave." He has begged many times to be allowed to go and live with his (the Suzulmus) family, although this has been generally discouraged. Even then, he takes them sweets, despite the fact that his family cannot afford it. Strange sacrifices for a child so young.

Ismail's obsession with Abeit has even penetrated his sleep. Often he has been heard crying out, "Gulsarin! Gulsarin!" and awakened showing great emotion. It is hard to imagine that anything other than deeply seeded factual experiences could bring on such a display of concern, particularly when the subject is sleeping.

Professor H. N. Banerjee, editor of the *Journal of Parapsychology,* interviewed the boy and all concerned extensively and concluded that it seemed more certain than usual that this particular case had not arisen through any desire to defraud. Banerjee noted that the family had not sought any publicity for the case and had, in fact, resisted for a year and a half the boy's demands to go to Abeit Suzulmus' home. When Banerjee and the press arrived on the scene, the family of Ismail were most reluctant to cooperate. Reports of the case had not even reached the outside world until three years after Ismail had first visited Abeit's home.

Banerjee also reported that ill feelings had arisen between the two families involved. It would seem most unlikely that a fraud could be so ingeniously perpetrated when those involved are not on speaking terms with one another.

THE THIRD TIME AROUND

Those who truly believe in the reality of reincarnation feel that the case of Swarnlata Mishra adds heavy ammunition to their cause. Swarnlata, the daughter of no less a personage than the Vice-Chancellor of Saugor University and former Home Minister of Madya Pradesh, India, claimed verifiable memories of two lives when she was but 10 years old.

"My name is Biya," the small girl told her family. "I was born about 1900. I had four brothers and two sisters. One of my younger brothers was Babu."

"Babu," she later related, was her pet name for her younger brother, Hari Prasad Pathak, and was what she had always called him when they were at home.

Hari heard of the strange claims of the 10-year-old girl and decided to make a trip to the Mishra home in order that he might convince himself of their validity. His sister, Biya, had been dead for almost 20 years! He made the journey to Chhatarpur, in April, 1959.

Upon meeting the young girl, Hari questioned her regarding details of their childhood home, household articles, and many other family characteristics. As Hari stood in awe, the little girl told him not only of the location of their former home, but its size, color, and shape, as well. She recalled how their old home had been furnished inside, and she told him of many incidents that had happened decades before.

Chintamani Pandey, Biya's husband, and Murli Pandey, her son, also heard of Swarnlata's claims. They, too, were curious about this girl who said that she had lived a past life as mother of their family, so they traveled from Katni to Chhatarpur to see her.

Immediately Swarnlata recognized them both, expressing joy and asking of their well-being. When Chintamani produced an old group photo, she looked at it and smiled. "This is you, here, but you were much younger then."

Swarnlata was invited to the Pathak house for a visit, whereupon she was presented with some more group photographs, many of them quite old. From these, she easily identified her mother and father as well as two other brothers and an old servant.

Swarnlata's father, D. P. Mishra, recalls a family auto trip which they took when his daughter was about four years of age. As the car neared Katni (the childhood home of Biya), the child became very excited and asked the driver, "Take me to the house where I was born."

Little notice was taken of her remark until later. When they stopped at a roadside stand for tea, Swarnlata said, "We could take tea at my old house in Katni."

Her father dismissed her mutterings as nothing but childish babble and turned his attentions back to the trip.

The woman, Biya, died in 1939.

But there was no long time gap between Biya and Swarnlata. The 10-year-old daughter of a government official was to recall yet another life.

She told her parents that, that same year when Biya died, she was reborn into a Brahmin family at Silhatte in Assam State. In this life, her name was Kamlesh and her parents' names were Ramesh and Shashimata. They were people of means, for Kamlesh was taken to school each day in her own private automobile.

But the good life was not to last for her. One day, when she was nine years old, the car crashed into a tree fatally injuring her. She died in a hospital shortly after the accident.

Her father, D. P. Mishra, says that as early as the age of four, Swarnlata sang Assamese folk songs and performed Assamese tribal dances. Investigation has shown both the dances and the songs to be quite authentic, indeed strange in view of the fact that Swarnlata had never been outside the geographical boundaries of Madya Pradesh, nor, as her father confirms, had she ever come in contact with any Assamese.

H. P. Pastore, former president of the Municipal Board of Chhatapur, interviewed the girl, checking and verifying all other data, and came to the following conclusion:

". . . it is quite evident that, what she claims to recall, actually are memories of former lives."

THE EXECUTIONER LEFT HIS MARK

"I'm worried about our son," said Mrs. Hami to her husband. "He seems as if he were in another world. All he does all day long is wander around the house talking to himself."

"But it's common for young children to go around babbling." H. A. Tileratne Hami had no fears for his child. The woman's worries were obviously unfounded.

But the mother was not to pass it off that easily. For days she followed the two-year-old around the house, listening to him. Gradually, in bits and pieces, she picked up the gist of what he was saying.

Wijeratne was talking about another life! He muttered to himself about his arm being deformed because he had murdered his wife in his former life. The Laws of Karma were doing their justice.

Mrs. Hami immediately recalled a conversation which she had had earlier with her husband in which she remembered his commenting that there were marked similarities between his son, Wijeratne, and his deceased brother, Ratran Hami. Even later when her husband had said, "This is my brother come back," she had not paid much attention to it. Now she began to wonder.

She told her husband of what the boy had said concerning the murder of his "wife," and she asked him questions about Ratram Hami, a subject hitherto unmentioned in the household. H. A. Tileratne had always been vague in reference to his brother. Now, with the question put to him and the overwhelming evidence reiterated by his son, he told her the story.

Tileratne Hami and his brother Ratram Hami had been farmers in the village of Uggalkaltota at the time. Tileratne was some 15 years the elder, but it was Ratran who got married first. On October 14, 1927, Ratran and his wife, Podi Menike, had come to some disagreement. As a result of the argument, the bride refused to leave her parents' home and go with Ratran to his village. This angered Ratran to the extent that he drew forth his kris and assaulted the disobedient wife, subsequently killing her.

The murderous bridegroom was tried, convicted, and sentenced to hang. When the sentence of the court had been pronounced, Tileratne went to his brother and asked him if there were anything he could do.

Ratran replied, "I am not afraid. I know that I will have to die. I am only worried about you. Don't sorrow, my brother. I will return."

In July, 1928, Ratran was executed.

In August, 1961, Dr. Ian Stevenson and Francis Story interviewed Wijeratne with members of his family and were able to throw a little more light on the "why" of the case. Marriages in Ceylon are accomplished in two stages. When a marriage is agreed upon, usually by the parents of the families involved, a legal contract is drawn up. A delay may then occur before the formal wedding feast and the domestic union and consummation of the marriage. During the interval between legal marriage and wedding feast it is not uncommon for the bride to continue to live at her parents' home, but she must remain in readiness to depart with her husband when he calls for her. Such was the case of Ratran and Podi Menike. The legal ceremony had taken place, but the final ones were yet to come.

Wijeratne relates that he (Ratran-Wijeratne) feared

that his wife had become infatuated with another man, who had persuaded her not to go through with her marriage to Ratran. When it came time for the final step of the marriage, Ratran went to his wife's house to get her. She refused.

The bridegroom pleaded with her, but when Podi would not be swayed, he walked the five miles back to his own home. There he got out his knife and sharpened it. He returned to the house of Podi Menike and once again begged her to return with him to consummate their marriage.

Again Podi refused, and then Ratran saw that his beloved was in the company of his rival. Being thus angered, Ratran fell upon the wayward wife and ended her infidelity—and her life.

Wijeratne-Ratran says he definitely remembers the gallows and the sensations he underwent as the trap was sprung. It seemed as though he were dropping into a pit of fire. After that he forgot everything until he was two years old and realized that he had been reborn as his brother's son.

When he talks of the murder, Wijeratne states, "I had an unbearable temper at the time. I did not think of the punishment I would get." He continues, "But I do not think that I did wrong. If I were again faced with the situation of a disobedient wife, I think I would act as before."

How did a boy of two acquire such an enormous amount of exacting information about a past life and a past crime when, in fact, his mother had never known of the incident and his father had never mentioned his uncle's execution around the house? Ariyaratne, Wijeratne's older brother by seven years, verifies the fact that his father had never spoken of Ratran and that Wijeratne began to narrate the story in great detail when he was no more than two and a half years old!

Wijeratne has since given up spontaneously speaking of the subject, but will talk about it freely whenever it is mentioned.

In Volume XXVI, *Proceedings.* of the American Society for Psychical Research, September, 1966, (*Twenty Cases Suggestive of Reincarnation*), Dr. Ian Stevenson concludes his investigation by commenting on Wijeratne's statement that, as Ratran Hami, he had killed Podi Menike and, in similar circumstances, he would not hesitate to kill her again. The researcher points out that Ratran Hami pleaded innocent at his trial. Stevenson seems inclined to believe that this difference supports the reincarnation hypothesis as opposed to the theory that Wijeratne obtained his information through extrasensory perception from his parents or, conceivably, from the court records. Investigator Stevenson feels that if Wijeratne had acquired his information from these sources, he would have adhered to the plea of "not guilty."

DOES THIS BOY PROVE REINCARNATION?

She was somewhat less than three years old when little Gnanatilleka Appuhamy began speaking of a former life.

One day when her mother was returned to the house with a bundle of kindling for the kitchen fire the little girl asked her, "Were the sticks free?"

When her mother replied that they were, the girl made the comment, "When I lived in Talawakelle, we had to buy wood for our kitchen fire."

What was this coming from the mouth of a child so young? A hint of a former life? Quizzed further, Gnanatilleka told her mother of how, in her previous life—when she was Turin Tillekeratne—she did many things which she remembered. The infant furnished details of the location and appearance of her former house in Talawakelle—the Post Office where her father had worked, a mountain which she supposedly had climbed, and of how she had seen Queen Elizabeth when her majesty had toured Ceylon in 1954.

Was little Gnanatilleka creating some sort of fantastic, childish make-believe? Or, had she lived before? Because of the strong Buddhist influence on the island, as well as intense interest in matters affecting or concerned with its doctrines of reincarnation, any such claims of past lives are carefully investigated and substantiated. As news spread of her astonishing claims, interviewers and investigators were attracted from many areas. One particularly interested party was the Ceylonese government itself!

Born in March of 1956, the daughter of D. B. D. Appuhamy, a farmer from the village of Kotmale, Gnanatilleka claims that in her previous life she occupied the person of Turin Tillekeratne, the son of G. Podiappuhamy, an officer in the Ceylonese Post Office, living in the village of Talawakelle. Turin Tillekeratne was born on January 1, 1941 and died November 9, 1954.

With this background data in mind, investigators proceeded to devise means to test the claims of Gnanatilleka. Although Kotmale and Talawakelle are only 20 miles apart, researchers were able to establish that she, Gnanatilleka, had never been to Talawakelle prior to her claims of a previous life in that area, and, although her parents had visited there, they did not know the family of Turin Tillekeratne.

For their first test, investigators under the direction

of H. S. S. Nisanka brought Turin's mother to a busy, crowded street in the village of Kandy, a major town in the tea region. They asked the woman to stand near a store while they brought Gnanatilleka down the street to see if the girl would recognize the mother of Turin.

While her father carried her down that same busy street, amidst the crowds of people, Gnanatilleka suddenly became excited and cried out, "Stop, stop! There stands my Talawakelle mother!"

To the amazement of the investigators, the girl had identified Turin's mother—a woman she had never met—from the midst of the crowded marketplace.

For another test, she was confronted with a group of people and asked to pick out her (Turin's) brothers and sisters. This she did without error, even calling them by their pet names!

Later on, while talking with them, she astonished them by relating personal incidents that had taken place between her and members of her family during Turin's lifetime. In particular, she told of the visit of Queen Elizabeth to the island. She and her brothers and sisters had run down to the railroad tracks to view the Queen as she passed. Their mother had stayed behind to watch from the house. This, according to the other members of Turin's family, was substantially correct. To their amazement the girl also told them of an incident where one of them had once been bitten by a dog. This, according to the family, was also correct.

And little Gnanatilleka continued, putting together pieces of Turin's life that had been all but forgotten for many years.

She spoke of school life at Sri Pada College in Hatton. The headmaster of this school confirmed that a boy named Turin Tillerkeratne had once attended there and that Gnanatilleka's details concerning the place were essentially accurate.

The tests convinced the chief investigator H. S. S. Nissanka that Gnanatilleka's story was no fabrication. Of the case he says, "I have no doubt that Gnanatilleka's is another genuine case of re-birth, of reincarnation."

The Podiappuhamy family has also come to that same conclusion. Of the girl, they comment, "There is no use going into details. We have studied Gnanatilleka closely, and we know that she is our son Turin."

Could the girl have made up the whole story? From the facts we have, it is not likely. Although she had never been to the village of Talawakelle, or, for that matter, had never heard anyone speak of the place, she was nonetheless able to tell investigators where Turin had lived, what his house had looked like, and to identify his mother, brothers and sisters.

She knew that, in Talawakelle, her mother had to buy firewood. While this is the case in most Ceylonese homes, Gnanatilleka could not have possibly known this fact, for in Kotmale, her family lived on a farm which bordered on a woodlot where they always had access to plenty of free firewood. Gnanatilleka had never seen a wood vendor in her area.

The same situation is true of coconuts. In Kotmale there are many trees and coconuts are plentiful, but in Talawakelle, all of the land is taken up by the tea-growing plantations and it is necessary to buy coconuts there. She knew this, yet she had never been there, nor had she ever heard anyone speak of it.

Gnanatilleka's story of the mountain climb prompted further investigation. While it is quite common for a Buddhist youth to make a pilgrimage up Adam's Peak, (for here it is said that the Lord Buddha left the imprint of one of his feet), it was found that the girl's memories of the trip corresponded to those of Turin and were not just common knowledge events that might have been picked up by eavesdropping on other pilgrims.

Writing for United Press Internation, Joe Segera interviewed the girl personally. Concerning the interview, he writes, "I spoke to her in Sinhalese, an Aryan language spoken by the majority race that inhabits Ceylon, the Sinhalese . . . my general observation of this peasant girl made during our conversation is that she is a very intelligent girl for her age. For a child who was not yet six when I interviewed her, it was remarkable to hear her speak the Sinhalese language so fluently and unfalteringly . . . this evidence of reincarnation already has been accepted by thousands of Ceylonese who have made pilgrimages to see and come away believing. . . ."

RETURN OF THE MURDERED HEIR

"Where are all of my toys?" demanded the small boy.

"Your toys are right there where you always keep them," replied his mother rather sternly.

"Not these," he persisted. "The other ones!"

"Oh, Ravi," moaned his sister, "don't start that again!"

The "that" that Ravi Shankar* was about to start again was the story of his previous life as Munna, son of Sri Jageshwar Prasad. This existence, Ravi claimed, had ended abruptly on January 19, 1951, when he had been lured away from his house and murdered by two men.

Ravi-Munna (Munna was a nickname for Ahsoka-

---

* No relation to the world-famous sitar virtuoso.

mar), was playing outside that day when two men came up to him and offered him a few coins—which to a six-year-old, must have seemed like a King's ransom—if he would only accompany them. There seemed to be no harm in going with the men. After all, one of them was a relative, so what could possibly happen? Besides, a new toy every once in a while never hurt anyone.

His eyes filled with visions of great reward, young Munna left what he had been doing and accompanied the men. He was not alarmed when they changed their direction and headed toward the river. Perhaps it was a boat which the men were going to give him.

When they reached the river, the men turned on him.

"And now you'll be out of my way," his relative said.

As the boy stared at them in startled disbelief, the men produced weapons and murdered him, removing his head and severely mutilating the rest of his body.

The murderers, a barber and a washerman, were later arrested. They had been seen in the area in the company of young Munna. The motive for the murder was assumed to be the elimination of Prasad's heir so that the relative might receive the property. With this testimony leveled against them, one of the men made a confession. But after they had been officially charged, he retracted his statement, thus destroying the case for the state. There had been no witnesses to the crime and so, for lack of evidence, the case had to be dropped and the confessed murderers were set free.

Six months later, in another district, Ravi was born. From the time that he was between two and three years old, he began telling, with remarkable accuracy, the story of Munna.

Word of the claims reached Sri Jageshwar Prasad,

Munna's father, and he went to see Ravi with the idea of either corroborating or refuting the boy's story.

Ravi's father, Sri Babu Ram Gupta, was quite annoyed at Prasad's mission, fearing that the man was somehow plotting to take the boy from him, and he refused to let Prasad see the child. Sri Prasad, however, arranged an audience with Ravi's mother, and through her, was permitted a confrontation with the boy.

Ravi's account of the murder was substantially the same as that which Sri Prasad and the investigating officials had been able to put together. The confession of the one murderer lent even further credence to the story.

Sri Prasad was so impressed with the boy's statements that he tried to re-open the case against the murderers of his son. For some reason, possibly due to the unacceptability of Ravi's testimony, this was not possible.

Ravi's father became even more annoyed with the situation as more and more investigators called upon the boy and more questions were put to him. Sri Babu Ram Gupta discouraged the boy from talking about his alleged memories of Munna's life any further and beat him when he did. Gupta went so far as to send Ravi out of the district for a while, in hopes that local interest would die down, and Ravi would forget about his past life.

Sri Ram Gupta, protective as his interests were, would never have the last word. Shortly after Ravi returned from his paternally inflicted exile, his father died.

Of particular interest is the congenital marking on the neck of Ravi Shankar, which gives an appearance of being an old scar from a healed knife wound. Is it possible that this might be a reminder of the murder in his past life?

Also noteworthy is the fact that Ravi still fears the

two men who allegedly killed Munna. He does not know the men nor why he fears them, Ravi told investigator Dr. Ian Stevenson in 1962, but whenever he meets them on the street or elsewhere, he gets shudders in his body and a certain feeling of anxiety.

As Ravi gets older, the memories of Munna are fading from him. Little regarding the murder is clear to him anymore, but his memory seems to improve when stimulated in conversation and he can recall a great deal then. Perhaps this tendency toward repression stems from Ravi's father's attempts to make the boy forget Munna and his past life.

THE PAST LIFE OF BHAJAN SINGH

Thakur Netrapal Singh's mind was heavy with thought as he traveled the road from Chandgari to Jamalpur, India.

Was his grandson Munesh going insane? Was the boy just babbling?

Singh dismissed both these ideas as he made his way through the night. Young Munesh was too sincere to be making the story up. And he had repeated the facts too many times.

"I am Bhajan Singh.* I belong to the village of Itarni. I have a wife, three brothers, a mother, and a daughter." The boy had rambled on about his possessions, his home, and his family.

---

* Singh is as common a name in India as Smith is in the U.S.

Thakur Netrapal Singh would find out once and for all. Itarni was on his way. He would stop and inquire around. Perhaps someone there had heard of Bhajan Singh.

He had not been in Itarni long when he discovered that there had been a man named Bhajan Singh but that the man had died from the fever in 1951, leaving a wife and a daughter. Munesh had been born in 1951!

The grandfather sought out Bhajan Singh's family and told them of how his four-year-old grandson, Munesh, kept insisting that he was Bhajan Singh.

The family was, quite naturally, curious to hear of this. A few days later a brother, Bhure Singh, and his brother-in-law, journeyed to Chandgari to see Munesh and talk to him.

Upon seeing the two men, Munesh began to weep. When asked by his grandfather to identify them, he pointed to Bhure and called him by name. The two visitors quizzed Munesh for a time, and then prepared to leave.

As they were about to depart, Munesh grabbed Bhure's arm. "Take me with you," he pleaded. "I want to go home to Itarni."

Only when the grandfather agreed to take Munesh there to visit did the boy quiet down.

Word of the boy's alleged reincarnation reached Ayodhya Devi, Bahjan Singh's widow. Curious, she and her sister-in-law made plans to visit Chandgari and the boy, Munesh. When they arrived, both women were dressed alike, with veils over their faces. Munesh began to weep again, recognizing them immediately.

But tears were not enough to convince the widow. Ayodhya Devi arranged to be alone with Munesh, then asked him to relate some specific event in their married life that would prove to her that he was indeed her husband reborn.

Munesh replied that he had beaten her one time with a churning stick and had cut her arm. The four-year-old went on to tell the woman of their marital relations, secrets that are spoken of only between husband and wife in India.

Such intimate revelations convinced Ayodhya Devi, and she asked that Munesh be allowed to go with her to Itarni. The boy's parents agreed, and Ayodhya Devi and the four-year-old reincarnation of her husband set out on the 40-mile trip the next morning.

As the strangely reunited couple neared Itarni, they were met by a crowd of villagers. Munesh looked over the crowd rather matter of factly, not being particularly excited by the reception. Then he saw his (Bahjan Singh's) best friend standing amid the crowd.

"Bhagwati Prasad!" he yelled, and Ayodhya Devi stopped the cart. The two "friends" spoke to each other about events of the past, and when they had finished, Bhagwati Prasad was certain that Munesh was his old friend, Bhajan Singh.

Munesh then led the crowd directly to Bhajan Singh's house (Munesh had never been there before), when he saw Bhajan's mother. At this he was overjoyed and broke into tears again.

When Munesh-Bhajan had regained control of his emotions, he took the crowd on a tour of the farm, answering questions and pointing out things of interest which he remembered well.

The four-year-old boy then showed them the house and the attic which had been his room. Munesh-Bhajan told the astonished crowd how he had spent his wedding night there and also how he had died there.

Before he left, Munesh had identified all of his former

possessions—his will, his garden, four bullocks, and two buffalo.

When Munesh had returned to his home in Chandgari, he became lonesome and longed for the company of his wife, Ayodhya Devi, and his daughter. He had not yet seen his daughter in his present life as Munesh, and he begged his grandfather to let him go to her. After much persuasion, it was agreed, but this time no foreknowledge of Munesh's arrival was given.

Nevertheless, as before, Munesh-Bhajan walked directly to the house of his father-in-law, as if he had been there many times. He seemed to recognize everyone there, but his happiest moment came when they presented his daughter. Bhajan was so taken with seeing her again that he would not leave her side and even refused to eat unless she were present.

Presently, Munesh-Bhajan had to go back to Chandgari; but there he was very unhappy, and the only time he showed joy or enthusiasm was when one of his (Bhajan Singh's), family visited him. Whenever they left, the boy would grieve over their departure. Munesh's past life so possessed him that it seemed to completely overshadow the present world.

Could four-year-old Munesh have fabricated the fantastic story? Was his family engaged in some kind of gigantic hoax? It is highly unlikely. When Munesh first began to speak of a previous life, he was mocked and ridiculed, even punished when he persisted in telling his "stories." There was no attempt at monetary gain made by any member of either family. World notoriety seems a remote possibility as a motive, for other than word of mouth gossip, the case was not published in even the local paper for nearly four years after Munesh had begun to make his claims.

What seems even more conclusive, is the overwhelming evidence that there was no normal way in which

Munesh could have obtained the information which he expounded. Forty miles between villages is a formidable distance in India, and communication is very poor. Munesh had rarely been out of his own village, and when he had, he had been accompanied by a member of his own family. Moreover, no one in Munesh's village of Chandgari had ever heard of Bhajan Singh. Bhajan's obituary had never even been printed in the newspapers!

Hemendra Nath Banerjee, professor of philosophy, Government College, Sri Ganganagar, India, an authority on extra-sensory perception among children, conducted an extensive investigation of the case. Writing in *Fate*, Banerjee says:

"We have checked, cross-checked, double-checked and triple-checked, and still we come to the same conclusion. This is a case of extra-cerebral memory.

"This term is a working term for us. We do not wish to say 'reincarnation' or 'multiple personality' or 'spirit possession' for we, as empirical scientists, shy away from occult and spiritualistic connotations.

"Our term only means that Munesh's claims of memories of a past life appear to be independent of the cerebrum, the seat of memory in the brain, which is thought to die at the death of the individual."

What, then, have the parapsychologists concluded in the case of Munesh?

"Only that we do not know," Banerjee admits.

THE POISON VICTIM CAME BACK

"Jasbir has died of smallpox," Sri Girdhari Lai Jat said to his brother, Sri Paltu Singh. "Will you come and help me bury him?"

"But it's late, Girdhari," answered the brother. "Why not wait until morning?"

Girdhari agreed disconsolately. It was getting late. Perhaps morning would be a better time to consider such a task. He returned home to the side of his three-and-a-half year old son, Jasbir. The night would be long. What more could he do here? Would he not better serve his own needs by getting some sleep? But, alas, he had a duty to his son.

A few hours later, as Girdhari was looking at the small, still figure lying on the bed, he thought he saw his son's body move. Impossible!

He continued staring at the corpse.

There it was again! His son was not dead!

Jasbir convalesced for several weeks before he finally regained his power of speech. When he did, Jasbir was not the same boy. Somehow, during his coma, he had undergone a complete transformation of character. Jasbir now thought of himself as Sobha Ram, son of Shankar of Vehedi village, and he expressed a strong desire to go there and be with his father and family.

He refused to eat food in the Jat household on the grounds that he was a Brahmin, a higher caste, and that such an act was unthinkable and taboo in the light of the rules of caste.

Sri Girdhari Lal Jat was at a loss as to what to do. If he did not take food, Jasbir would die for certain. But how could he force the boy to eat? How could he convince the boy that he was not a Brahmin?

A neighbor who was a Brahmin, heard of Girdhari's plight, and lent a helping hand. She cooked for Jasbir in the Brahmin manner, from foodstuffs which Girdhari supplied. This she did for almost two years.

However, during the same period of time, unbeknownst to Jasbir, the boy was also eating food from the table of his father. Little by little the Jat family had been substituting food from the same menu from which they fed.

When Jasbir discovered the deception, he wanted no more to do with it, but the family put pressure on him, stating that he had already violated the taboos and eaten the food of a lower caste. Eventually, they talked Jasbir into giving up, at least temporarily, his rigid Brahmin dietary habits and taking regular meals with them. This Jasbir did, but he did not give up his obsession with the new personality. He was Sobha Ram, and he continued to give the family details of his life and death.

He died, he said, in the village of Vehedi, following a wedding procession. According to Jasbir (Sobha), he had eaten some sweets during the procession between villages. The sweets were allegedly given to him by a man to whom he had lent money in the past. In an effort to avoid his debts, the man had poisoned Sobha.

Somewhere along the road between Nirmana and Vehedi, Sobha had become dizzy and nauseated and had fallen from his chariot, suffering a severe head injury. A few hours later he died in Vehedi.

The Jat family desired no notoriety in connection with their son Jasbir, so they tried to keep his babblings as quiet as possible. Word, however, was eventually to leak out.

A Brahmin lady, while visiting in Rasulpur, had heard via the Brahmin circles of the special cooking that had been done for the boy Jasbir. The lady, Srimati Shyamo, was a native of Rasulpur, but she had married a native of Vehedi and had since lived there.

She was quite naturally curious, when, on one of her visits to Rasulpur, Jasbir seemed to recognize her. From then on, it was only a matter of inquiry before Srimati Shyamo learned of the boy's strange story.

The story of Jasbir, corresponded almost identically with that of one Sobha Ram, a young man of 22, whom she had known in Vehedi. Sobha Ram had been a son of the Tyagi family, who were friends of hers. Sobha had died recently in a chariot accident, similar to the one which Jasbir had described.

Srimati Shyamo took this story to the Tyagi family, who were very much interested in the information their friend had acquired, for as far as they had known, Sobha had died directly as a result of injuries sustained in the chariot accident. They knew nothing of Sobha's debtor or of any poisoning.

They traveled to Rasulpur to hear Jasbir's story directly from the boy. Jasbir recognized each member of the family immediately and expressed his affection and his appreciation of their visit.

Under questioning, he related to them detailed events of the life of Sobha, all of which were corroborated by the family. He showed a special affection toward Baleshwar, the son of Sobha Ram.

On a later occasion, Jasbir was taken to Vehedi and put down near the railway station. He was then told to lead the party to the Tyagi quadrangle. This task he accomplished without difficulty. To confirm the boy's phenomenal sense of familiarity with Vehedi, Jasbir was next taken to the home of Sri Ravi Dutt Sukla. From there he once again led the procession back to the Tyagi quadrangle without making a wrong turn.

It should be noted that, although the villages of Rasulpur and Vehedi are but twenty or so miles apart, they are off the beaten track, and communication between them is quite poor. Few residents of either town have ever had occasion to visit the other. It was clearly established that any information Jasbir had concerning the Tyagi family would have to have been obtained by other than normal means.

Jasbir seems quite happy when in Vehedi and he has developed a strong personal committment to the Tyagi family. When he is at home in Rasulpur, he seems lonely and unhappy. Consequently, the Jat family have tried to discourage the boy from speaking of a life as Sobhar. They have refused to let him visit Vehedi, and they have prevented him from meeting the wife of Sobha Ram, since such a confrontation might further sever his ties with his present family.

REINCARNATION AND ESP

"Shanti's talking about her husband again," a playmate teased the small girl.

"But I do have a husband," the little girl protested. "And a son, too."

The more the girl insisted, the more laughter came from the children around her on the streets of Delhi, the old capital city of India. She had become used to mockery for telling about the things she remembered. Even her parents had warned Shanti not to talk of her "husband" and "son" so much. But sometimes the feelings within her little body were so strong that she could not keep them inside.

Shanti Devi, from her earliest childhood, claimed to remember details from a life lived in the city of Muttra. Most of her family and relatives ignored the girl's claims to such knowledge and attributed the intimate descriptions of the place where she claimed to have grown up and lived to the over-active imagination of a child.

By sheer persistence, Shanti aroused the curiosity of Professor Kishen Chand, her granduncle. To satisfy himself and, perhaps to put an end to Shanti Devi's claim on the husband she had in Muttra, the professor detailed the information that he had gained from listening to the girl and sent a letter off to a man named Kedar Nath Chaubey, whom Shanti Devi contended had been her husband in Muttra.

Professor Chand was more than a little surprised when he received an answer from such a man in Muttra. Shanti had never been near the city of Muttra, yet she had given him not only the correct name of the man whom she contended was her husband, but also the correct address of his house. Chand was not one for arriving at premature conclusions, but he had to admit that these were at least very strange coincidences.

Kedar Nath Chaubey, the man who received the letter, was puzzled, too. He had a son, but his wife had died nine years before. Cautiously, Chaubey decided not to go to Delhi himself to talk to Professor Chand, but to send a friend to find out if some attempt were being made to defraud him. After the friend had contacted Shanti's parents, he wrote to Kedar Nath that the case merited some investigation, for the little girl came from a respected family.

Kedar Nath and his son traveled to Delhi to meet Professor Chand and Shanti Devi. Still openly skeptical about the truth of the story that had been related to him, Chaubey was amazed to find that the girl knew things about him that only his former wife might know.

Shanti went directly to the man's son, embraced him, and spoke to him in the terms of endearment that his wife had used nine years before! She also assumed the same attitude toward him that his wife had taken before her death. The next day, Chaubey left Delhi in great confusion, in spite of the protests of Shanti Devi that she wished her "son" to stay with her.

Desh Bandhu Gupta, then president of the All-India Newspaper Editors' Conference, as well as a member of parliament, prepared a scheme which he thought would determine the validity of Shanti's claims. Mr. Gupta, and other prominent people interested in the case, escorted Shanti Devi by train to Muttra. The girl was then asked to direct the party to the house in which she had lived with her husband.

The instructions Shanti Devi gave were clear and precise and she led the party unerringly through the narrow streets of Muttra to the front door of a dwelling.

"I used to live in this house," she said to the men. "But when I lived here the building was painted yellow."

The men looked at the white exterior of the building then back at the girl. One of them knocked at the door of the dwelling.

To the girl's surprise, the occupant of the house was not Kedar Nath and his son, but a family unknown to her. The skeptics in the crowd thought that they had finally caught the girl in her deception, but Shanti asked if she could be taken to where her "husband" lived.

Kedar Nath listened to the story and confirmed that the house that the girl had led the crowd to had been his nine years before. He explained that, shortly after the death of his wife, he had moved to a smaller dwelling. The first letter from Professor Chand had been forwarded to him from the old address.

To prove her contention that she did remember a past life as Kedar Nath's wife, Shanti led the party of investigators to her "mother's" house. Once again she did not err in her directions. Mr. Gupta asked the girl if she noticed anything different about the building, as she had noticed the difference in paint on the former house of her "husband." After looking about briefly, she told them that there had been a well located in a certain corner of the property. The ground was turned over, and the casing of a long unused well was uncovered. Even the most skeptical in the group began to wonder what strange powers the girl possessed.

Shanti Devi found her "mother" inside the house and identified her immediately, though the old woman was withered and bent with age. The group of men could no longer deny the validity of the girl's claims. They signed statements that testified to what they had seen, and these, together with the testimonies of Kedar Nath Chaubey, and the girl's parents, were enough to create an immediate sensation in the Indian press.

Could some facet of extrasensory perception explain the well-known case of Shanti Devi cited above?

If it were telepathy which provided Shanti Devi with her information, then her ESP abilities must have been developed to a degree that would enable her to perceive messages from a distant city about a woman who had been dead for nearly a decade. There must be agents who "broadcast" the impressions which a telepathic percipient receives. A great many people in Muttra must have had Kedar Nath's wife on their minds at all times. That a simple housewife had made such a great impression upon the citizens of Muttra is too preposterous an assumption to follow.

Once Shanti Devi was brought to Muttra, however, one might make a case for the hypothesis that the girl was drawing her knowledge from the subconscious minds of Kedar Nath, his son, and his friends. The impressive fact that Shanti Devi often described things as they had been nine years before, rather than as they were at the present, may also be attributed to telepathic reception of information from the subconscious of the many people who crowded about her.

But even in Muttra, the telepathic hypothesis becomes stretched to the snapping point. To be able to accomplish such apparent feats of memory via some extrasensory ability, Shanti Devi would have had to have the ability to probe the minds of Kedar Nath and the other assembled adults, discard what was contemporary, determine which impressions denoted past conditions, and arrive at a subconscious consensus, all in the split second which it took her to respond to the questions put to her by her interrogators. The girl could have made a fortune as a professional medium! Clearly, there is something more at work in the Shanti Devi case than ESP.

I find the extrasensory hypothesis useful in explaining many cases suggestive of reincarnation, however. Take, for example, the well attested to phenomenon of retrocognition, the "psi" experience wherein one perceives a scene from the past and thereby derives information about a past event which he could not have acquired through normal means.

It seems to me that retrocognition could account for such an experience as the businessman, whom we discussed in an earlier chapter, who felt himself an Indian while camping with his boy scouts. Perhaps he perceived a scene from the past when Indians did indeed lie sleeping outside of Indian Cave. As he lay there in a semi-trancelike state, some part of his subconscious may have dramatized the incident to include him as a character within the scene instead of being merely the percipient. To illustrate with an example, we have all had the experience of incorporating the ringing of the alarm clock into our dreams. Tickle the foot of a sleeper and his dream machinery may transform that sensation into the caress of a lovely maid or the slither of a deadly reptile, depending upon some unknown whim of the subconscious.

Then, too, our young student, who so stubbornly insisted that a room lay beyond the stone wall in the German castle, may have been sensitive to certain vibrations in the psychic ether and have "seen" through the stone via retrocognition. To offer another ESP-oriented explanation of this case, the student may have clairvoyantly perceived the information of the hidden room from either the ancient book in the curator's office or from the forgotten memories of the curator himself.

Admittedly, the ESP hypothesis is qute unsatisfactory in explaining many of the documented cases with which we have dealt in this book, but by the same token, one should not accept every strange flash of "memory" as proof of reincarnation. An unfamiliar room may seem to evoke hidden memories because of its own peculiar atmosphere or because scenes of violent emotional impact have been enacted within its walls. An old stone axe may seem to trigger a flood of memories because of a latent psychometric talent on the part of the individual who touches its surface. But in each of these ESP-induced experiences, the percipient is observing, not remembering.

It seems to me that it was ESP at work rather than a manifestation of reincarnation in this case quoted by Rev. Leslie D. Weatherhead in his *The Case of Reincarnation*.

According to Rev. Weatherhead, in October of 1959, he received a letter from a woman who had a university degree in science but who had had no interest in matters of a psychic nature until after her son's early death. The woman tells of a number of unusual experiences which her son David had during his brief life span.

"From four years he spoke of an invisible playmate —whom he called his Little Princess. In any difficulty, he would say: 'I must ask my Little Princess.' "

Rev. Weatherhead's correspondent says that she and her husband identified the invisible visiting royalty with her husband's ancestors, ". . . and do indeed believe he could see and hear her."

At age seven, according to the woman, David accompanied her to Rome to visit her grandmother, who stayed in Italy a great deal. For an afternoon's outing, the woman and her son accompanied a noted archaeologist to view a recently excavated Roman villa on the outskirts of Naples.

From the moment they reached the excavation, David became very emotional and excited and ran about the ruins until he came to a Roman bath engraved with the signs of the Zodiac.

"Here's our bath, and our tiles—mine had a bull on it and the fish was Marcus," the boy shouted excitedly.

"As he said the name 'Marcus,' " the woman writes, "he burst into floods of tears and called out: 'Take me away—it was all so terrible, I can't bear it.' "

Another of David's strange experiences took place when he and his parents were visiting some caves in Guernsey, which had been used at one time as prisons for French soldiers. The boy began to tap on the walls of the cave and told his parents that there was yet another cave where a young prisoner had been walled in.

David told his skeptics that he had "watched it being done."

The authorities denied the existence of such a cave and the perpetration of such an act.

Then David gave the name of the prisoner, and his parents insisted upon a closer examination of the records by the authorities.

"Eventually, steps were taken and the walls were tapped for any thin place which could have been the outline of a door. The door was found: it had been bricked up. Stretched out on the floor was the skeleton of a man. When the archives were searched, the name David had given was correct."

When David was 14, his mother accompanied him to look at some new mummies which had been acquired by the British Museum. His mother felt she would be asking for yet another of David's flights into the unknown, but, to her surprise, her son appeared quite calm.

His calm, it appears, was deceptive. After he had peered inside a sarcophagus, David complained that there should have been three initials on the underside of the case.

His mother asked him if he could draw the initials, and David made three birds on his note pad.

"That was my name," he told her, "but you weren't

there then. I was a kind of inspector; I had to mark the coffins if they were satisfactory."

Rev. Weatherhead concludes that such strange happenings have "no adequate interpretation other than that of reincarnation."

It seems much more likely to me that young David was an exceptionally gifted clairvoyant. Such people as Peter Hurkos, Croiset, and my good friend, John Pendragon, have the extraordinary talent of being able to hold scarves, watches, rings, letters, and other items and thereupon being able to recite episodes of the owners' past, present, and, sometimes, his future.

Such emotion-charged places and objects as an ancient Roman villa, a prison cave, and an Egyptian mummy would seem to be powerful broadcasters to the sensitive psyche of a young clairvoyant. Again, perhaps because of his youth and his inability to understand his ESP talents, David may have projected himself into the impressions which he perceived when he came into contact with certain places and things. When such an exceptionally talented clairvoyant as Great Britain's John Pendragon receives emanations from an object or letter, he perceives the impressions of his "psychic screen," almost as if he were watching a television drama unfold. Only under the most unusual of circumstances would a clairvoyant feel himself caught up in the impressions or feel himself a part of the drama.

Another strike which I would call on the interpretation of David's experiences as being suggestive of reincarnation is the matter of the great coincidence of the young man happening to encounter such widely separated locales for his former lives in his own brief, life span.

It would seem to me to be stretching the laws of chance a bit far to consider that a young boy from

London could happen to arrive in Naples just as his former villa was being excavated, tour the caves in Guernsey where he had served either as guard or prisoner, and happen to come into contact with the one sarcophagus among thousands that contained the bandaged earthly shell of a former life. No, it seems much more realistic to suppose that David and his parents were unaware of the fact that he was possessed of a great talent for psychometry.

ESP, then, in this writer's opinion, may account for many alleged cases of reincarnation. One little-understood phenomenon may not be used to explain away the existence of another, however, and extrasensory perception as a general hypothesis to account for all cases suggestive of reincarnation, admittedly, does not stand the test.

THE MAN WHO IS HIS OWN UNCLE

Phoh looked around the crowd of irate villagers who surrounded him. He was silent.

"Cattle thief!" one of them shouted.

Phoh turned his head to refute the accusation. At that instant a knife whistled through the air, piercing the back of his skull. Phoh was dead by the time he hit the ground.

But what is death?

Phoh could see his body lying there on the ground, blood gushing from the knife wound. He wanted to go back to it, but he feared all the people standing around. Perhaps they would try to kill him again.

Phoh did not return to his body. Instead, in this spirit-like form, he visited friends and relatives.

"I was very distraught when they could not see me or feel my hands when I would touch them."

When he arrived at his brother's house, Phoh found himself at breakfast with his sister-in-law, who also was unaware of his presence.

"She was heavy with child, and I was overcome by a certain compulsion to enter her body, which I did. I dwelled there for a few months, until it was time for her to deliver, then I emerged from her womb as Thiang."

This is the story told by Siamese Army Sgt. Thiang San Kla, the man who claims to be his Uncle Phoh, reborn.

Prior to his death, Phoh had been suffering from a suppurating wound on his right big toe. He also had been tatooed on both hands and feet, a protective measure which supposedly gave a man immunity from the weapons of his enemies.

When Thiang was born, just three months after Phoh's death in July, 1924, his right big toe was slightly deformed, and he had markings on his hands and feet which strongly resembled tatooing. On the left rear surface of his skull was a large birthmark, a capillary naevus, which corresponded exactly to the knife wound which Phoh had received.

It was not until he was about four years of age that Thiang began to relate his story. At that time, he told his parents that his name was Phoh and that he was his father's brother reborn.

Although Thiang's father only lived for two months after the boy had begun to talk, it was sufficient time to convince him that his young son was also his brother. Before he died, Thiang told him not only of many events concerning Phoh's life that he, as Phoh's brother would know, but also many things which he was able to verify through others.

Thiang-Phoh recognized and identified all of the members of both his and Phoh's families as well as many of Phoh's friends.

Phoh's wife, Pai, heard about the claims of her nephew and traveled from her home in the village of Ar Vud to Ru Sai, Thiang's home.

Although the two villages are but 25 kilometers apart, there is still relatively little communication between them. With her, Pai brought some items that had been Phoh's possessions, as well as a number of articles that had not.

Thiang correctly, and with apparent ease, separated the articles into two groups—those which had been his, and those which he had never seen before.

While this was quite a convincing display, Pai required more proof. Thiang readily obliged by taking her aside and recounting to her some of the more intimate details of her family life.

This more than convinced Pai that Thiang was her husband Phoh reborn. It also placed her in a rather awkward situation. Pai was not a married woman, for her husband had been killed, yet she felt that she could not consider herself a widow, either, because of the overwhelming evidence of Phoh's rebirth as Thiang. In solution to her problem, Pai became a Buddhist nun.

Nai Pramaun, of the Municipality Office in Surin, is an interesting witness of the case.

Pramaun had been a young man and an Assistant District Officer at the time of Phoh's murder and had investigated the alleged cattle thefts as well as the murder. Because he lived in the area, Pramaun had also heard of the claims of the small boy, and because of his acquaintance with the family through his investigations regarding Phoh's death, he went to see Thiang.

Thiang recognized Pramaun immediately and addressed him by name. Thiang-Phoh recalled for the officer the names of all who were present at the murder, including the murderer himself, a man named Chang.

When he had finished his interview, the investigator examined the marks on Thiang's body. Although there was no other physical similarity between the two personalities, Pramaun told investigator Francis Story, who wrote of the case for *Fate*, that the birthmark and other deformities corresponded precisely with those on Phoh.

Thiang's story about the murder, Pramaun said, was also substantially correct, with, however, one inconsistency. Phoh, claims Thiang, was wrongfully accused of stealing cattle, but according to Mr. Pramaun, Phoh was a notorious figure in the area, who had definitely engaged in cattle theft.

One very convincing piece of evidence on the part of Thiang occurred when he recognized some land as that which had belonged to him in his life as Phoh. Nobody had told Thiang of this property, yet he was able to describe, exactly, the circumstances under which Phoh had acquired the land. He considered going into court in an effort to regain his property, but he abandoned the idea when told that he had no chance of recovering the land under such bizarre circumstances.

Thiang's story is well known throughout the area in which he lives. The evidence is so convincing that no one doubts its validity. But for Thiang it remains a nightmare . . . a nightmare in which he must exist in life as his own uncle!

THE CASE FOR REINCARNATION*

An afterword by David D. Graham,
Publisher, *Infinity Newsletter*

If a clergyman, as recent as twenty-five years ago, dared to approach the subject of reincarnation in his sermon he would certainly have placed himself in a position that would have subjected him to ridicule, followed by dismissal, and perhaps, even a trial for heresy. We have had liberal ministers and religious writers for a number of years, dating back at least to the 19th century, but even the most zealous liberal of that time would not touch reincarnation with a ten-foot pole. (At least, not from the pulpit!)

One of the greatest influences, which encouraged a more liberal attitude on the part of certain contemporary theologians, was the discovery of the Essene Library, more commonly called the Dead Sea Scrolls, which are believed to be writings made by the Essenes, during the time that Jesus was on Earth. The Essenes were Reincarnationists.

Such modern writer-ministers as Dr. Lewis Dunnington and Dr. Marcus Bach have both written and lectured on the subject of reincarnation, in spite of the fact that both were trained in, and preached, orthodoxy in their earlier years in the pulpit. These men, through their years of research and study, were able

---

*adapted from *Eternal Journey* by David D. Graham.

to find a certain credibility in the theory of reincarnation, and were not afraid to discuss it openly, when most ministers were still treading easy on the subject, if discussing it at all.

Reincarnation is certainly not a new idea, nor one limited to Oriental thought, but one with a long history, almost as old as civilization itself. We find early records of reincarnation dating back to 2500 B.C. in China, and to the reign of Thutmose III fifteen hundred years before the birth of Jesus, antidating the earliest writings of Judaism. Archeological discoveries have shown that the priests of ancient Egypt taught of the passing of the Soul or *BA* through different bodies after the physical death. Ancient records in China have histories dating back forty-five hundred years that show that they, too, had a belief in rebirth, as taught by such philosophers as Lav-Tze and Chaang-Tze. Buddhism, founded in the 6th century B.C., had as its foundation a belief in reincarnation, which its millions of followers retain to this day.

It must be kept in mind that Egypt and China, which are the oldest civilizations (excluding the possibility of Atlantis, Mu, etc.), were the centers of ancient culture and philosophy, and formulated the science of that time. The earliest Israelites of 1225 B.C. found much Egyptian influence in their religion, as shown by the teachings of the great law-giver, Moses. Many parallels are seen between Hebrew laws and the ancient sayings of Ptah-Hotep of Egypt concerning the laws of Justice and Right.

Another early civilization, Greece, also borrowed from Egypt, and one of the greatest mathematicians and philosophers of the 6th century, B.C., Pythagoras, was a Reincarnationist. He believed in the Soul as a "thought of God" and he considered the physical body to be simply one of a succession of "receptacles" for the housing of the Soul.

A long list of ancient Greek thinkers followed Pythagoras and they included such illustrious names as Plato, Socrates, and Aristotle. In fact, it was St. Augustine who said, "The message of Plato, the purest and most luminous of all philosophy, has at least scattered the darkness of error, and now shines forth mainly in Plotinus, a Platonist so like his master that one would think they live together, or rather, since so long a period of time separates them, that Plato is born again in Plotinus."

St. Clement of Alexandria said, "We were in being long before the foundation of the world; we existed in the eye of God, for it is our destiny to live in Him. We are the reasonable creatures of Divine Word. Not for the first time does He show pity on us in our wonderings. He pities us from the very beginning."

Many Christians will continue to say that this is all right for the non-Christians but, if it is a basic part of the teachings of Jesus, why do we not have reference to it in the New Testament?

Well, first of all, let's remember that many of the early Christian writings were either lost over the years, or deliberately destroyed by the 4th century, A.D. (some being found in 1947 that escaped destruction, called the Dead Sea Scrolls). Such early Christians as Origen, a Reincarnationist, later found disfavor with the Church and was considered anathema because of his difference on such basic subjects as Original Sin, of which he said, "We do not sin because of the first man having sinned, but the first man sinned for the same reason that we do; because he was still a child in Spiritual Evolution, and we ourselves are far from having reached perfection."

Another quotation from Origen says, "The Soul, which

is immaterial and invisible in its nature exists in no material place without having a body suited to the nature of that place; accordingly, it at one time puts off one body, which was necessary before, but which is no longer adequate in its changed state and it exchanges it for a second."

Once again referring to St. Augustine, we find that he was a Platonist, who wrote in his *Confessions*, "Did I not live in another body before entering my mother's womb?"

Other early Church leaders who were Reincarnationists included Basilides, Tatian the Apologist, Valentinius, Porphyry, Manes, St. Jerome, St. Pamphilius, St. Gregory, Jamblichus, and Arthenagoras, as a partial list.

Now, let us go to a few Biblical statements made by Jesus which have managed to remain over the centuries. We find a classic example when Jesus came to the coast of Caesarea Philippi, and He said to His disciples, "Whom do men say that I, the Son of Man, am?"

Their answer was, "Some say thou art John the Baptist; some Elias; and others Jeramiah or one of the Prophets." (Matthew 16:13-14)

Jesus, you will note, did not rebuff them, or say that this was silly, since all but John the Baptist had long been put in their graves, for it is obvious that the idea of reincarnation was an accepted thing, and justified no comment.

At another time when Jesus and His disciples were walking they came across a blind man, and one of the disciples asked, "Master, who did sin, this man or his parents that he was born blind?"

"Neither," answered Jesus, "did this man sin nor his parents; but that the works of God should be made manifest in him." (John 9:1-4) This seems to refer to the man's karma, and how he was working out of it in his current incarnation.

At another time His disciples asked Him why the Scribes had said that Elias must first come, to which Jesus answered, "Elias truly shall first come, and restore all things. But, I say unto you that Elias has come already and they knew him not!" The disciples then understood that Jesus was referring to John the Baptist. (Matthew 17:10-13)

It seems rather obvious that reincarnation is necessary in our Spiritual Evolution, for Jesus said that to enter the Kingdom of God (Oneness) we must be perfect, even as our Heavenly Father is Perfect, and Final or Complete Perfection is not possible for most of us in a single lifetime of a few decades at most. This takes time and much learning, gained through many incarnations, which are designed as stepping stones on our way to the top of the mountain.

The information gained from the Dead Sea Scrolls is already having much effect on the teachings of religious leaders of all faiths. Many new findings will affect both the Jewish and Christian religions, as more translations are made public.

It may seem coincidental, but I believe that it is all a part of Divine Plan that the end of World War II, terminated by the use of atomic bombs, ushering in the Atomic and Space Age, occurred in the same year (1945) that the Dead Sea Scrolls were found. In other words, the time has come for some drastic changes in our concepts of things Cosmic.

The Nag-Hammadi scrolls give a very strong indication that Jesus was either an Essene, a student of the Essenes, or at least associated very closely with them during the "silent years" from twelve to thirty. It has also been speculated that Jesus studied in Egypt, India, and even Tibet, although very little evidence of this has been presented to date. There is, however, a very strong link between the teachings of Jesus and those of the Teacher of Righteousness, who according to the records, lived nearly a hundred years before the birth of Jesus.

Little has been known of the Essenes prior to the discovery of the scrolls, but it is indicated that they formed a very definite link between Judaism and Christianity, and at a later date, when fierce hatred raged between Jews and Christians (Jew and Gentile), the teachings of the Essenes were deleted from *both* Canons. As a result, neither group was willing to retain the Essenic teachings, and they were either lost or destroyed, with the exception of those recently found at Qumran.

As I pointed out earlier, it is generally believed that the Essenes were Reincarnationists, and the fact that their writings were destroyed by early Christians and Jews alike may account in part for the loss of the teaching of reincarnation in the New Testament, other than for the few examples given here.

The general idea behind reincarnation, and the thing that lends a practical aspect to it, is that, through a series of incarnations, we are able to gain Oneness or Final Perfection through working out our individual karmas. Our spiritual evolvement must take place, whether we believe in reincarnation or not, for the time must come when we put aside all carnal imperfection, for to enter the Kingdom we must be perfect!

It must be remembered that the spirit of each of us is ageless, just as young today as it was ten thousand years ago, and that each incarnation is designed to further develop it. Reincarnation, whether fact or fancy, is at least a logical hypothesis in view of our need for complete perfection.

In many parts of the Orient, a person's birthday is

calculated from the time of conception, rather than birth as we in the West record age. The reason behind this is that it is generally believed that the Soul or entity enters the body at the exact moment of conception. Other groups, primarily in the West, believe that the Soul does not enter the physical body until the time of birth, but hovers near the mother for some time in order to attune to her temperament and to prepare itself for entry into the physical world. Still others say that the Soul does not enter the body until we reach puberty. The actual time probably makes little difference, for it does not change the basic theory of reincarnation.

We have covered some of the historical background of reincarnation, so it is only logical to look now at what some of the modern thinkers and metaphysical groups consider logical in their search for Truth.

In the latter part of the 19th century, Charles Fillmore and his wife founded what eventually became known as Unity School of Christianity. He once said that the Western World looks upon reincarnation as a heathen doctrine, and that many people close the doors of their minds without waiting to find out what message it may have for them, interpreted in the Light of Truth.

This statement had a shocking effect on the churchmen of that day, but, as Marcus Bach wrote in an article in *Good Business*, a Unity publication, "Time has a way of bringing Truth into focus, and Truth has a way of eventually finding Time on its side. Truth or speculation, reincarnation is a lively topic these days, and is an indication that we are living more and more in the wonderful world of Spirit."

Charles Fillmore, in agreement with Albert Schweitzer, said that Christ released us from the bondage of Karmic Law, allowing us to make the most of each incarnation, and this is where Christian reincarnation differs from that of many Oriental religions, which hold to the idea that we must work out our Karmas according to mistakes of past lives, with no chance for immediate redemption. This accounts for the caste system of India which prevents the individual from rising above his station in life, as gained at birth.

I would like to mention here that we should not confuse the theory of reincarnation with that of transmigration, which is a common error among many. Transmigration is the belief that when we die we return to inhabit the body of a lower animal form, such as cattle, cats, etc. This belief is followed by a small group in India, but has not a foundation in Christian thinking, for it is not logical to think that God causes us to retrogress to lower animal forms from His finest creation. Transmigration does account for the reverence given animals in India.

A man who has served as a point of reference in many writings on psychical research is Edgar Cayce, who passed out of his last incarnation in 1945, but left behind a wealth of readings and research papers that are housed at the Association for Research and Enlightenment, which he founded at Virginia Beach, Virginia in 1931, and which today has over twelve hundred active participants throughout the world.

Cayce said that each soul enters the material plane, not by chance, but through Grace; the Mercy of a Loving Father. As to whether the soul is developed or retarded during these incarnations is left to the free-will of the individual as he lives through these faults or rises above them in our journey toward Oneness. Life is a purposeful experience, and the place in which a person finds himself is one in which he may use his present abilities, faults, failures, virtues in fulfilling the purpose for which the Soul decided to manifest in the three-dimensional plane.

Cayce pointed out that no soul is placed here accidently. We are all where we are today because we have "chosen" to be there in an effort to work out our development.

Edgar Cayce's son, Hugh Lynn, once asked if his father had ever found out how he developed his psychic powers, and he was given the answer in a life reading of Edgar Cayce which showed that during Cayce's earlier incarnation he had been wounded in battle and left in the field for dead. However, he had managed to live for several days, conscious and in extreme pain. He was not able to move or help himself in any way, having only his mind as a weapon against pain. Just prior to his physical death he had been able to elevate his mind beyond the reach of his body and its suffering, and since no achievement, good or bad, is ever lost, the ability to subdue the body and its feelings became a part of the pattern of his individuality, and he was later able to use this power in the physical body of Edgar Cayce.

Another writer who has gained a great amount of insight into the field of reincarnation is Fay M. Clark, author of *Beyond the Light*. His trips into Cosmic consciousness were made while under the influence of mescaline, and his answers to various questions were all tape recorded, and often in direct conflict with his thinking when fully conscious.

His trips "beyond the light" varied in length from a few minutes to almost one hour, and his return to physical consciousness was always voluntary.

Have you ever wondered why some people are born into wealthy families and have every comfort that life can offer, while others are born into dire poverty, with the proverbial "three strikes" against them? Why some have every advantage that money and social prestige can bestow, while others stumble along with little gain in life? Why some people live to extremely old age, while in another case a child is born, only to die within a few weeks or years, having accomplished nothing so far as one can tell?

The reason for this, according to some of the greatest metaphysical minds, is because this is but one of many lives or incarnations that we experience, and we can not judge this one life solely on its record, but rather as a part of a great Cosmic jigsaw puzzle, each incarnation representing a piece of it, but all of them eventually creating the whole picture: Final Perfection. Lessons must be learned on this, the Earth Plane, and living various roles is the method of doing so.

An example of this might be found in a case that I know of first-hand, in which a child, just a few years old, was killed by an auto when he ran out into the street in front of his home. His family had experienced many marital problems, created to a large extent by drinking on the part of both parents. When the boy was born, both gave up drinking and became good parents, and when the boy was killed, neither returned to the old drinking habit, for they realized that he was given to them in order to bring them together and away from their former habits. This is only conjecture, but could it be that this little fellow had but one more incarnation before Perfection, and his role was to bring one more person out of the depths of degradation in order to gain his At-Oneness? I would like to think so.

In our various lives we do all sorts of things, some good, some bad, and the conditions under which we live in this life are the direct results of things we did in past lives, combined with our own free will in this life.

No one "sends" us anywhere. We are where we are by our own doing. Stop and think this over, and in all honesty, you will have to answer affirmatively. "Whatsoever a man soweth, that shall he also reap!" Of all the Biblical quotations, none is truer. We may blame our parents, employers, the police, the government, and a multitude of other people and circumstances, but in the final analysis, it is ourselves we have to blame for every condition. Once we realize this, we can feel that we are on the road to gaining in our spiritual evolution. In other words, we are today the direct result of what we have been and have thought, the Universal Law of Cause and Effect.

Probably no single theme in the teachings of Jesus is more important than that of Love. It must be kept in mind that like attracts like and we are continually drawn to others with whom we have strong emotional links, whether in love or hatred! For this reason we must completely eliminate all feelings of antipathy toward others. We must not only release ourselves but them. The key is Love, but if we cannot in all sincerity "love" our enemies, we must at least learn to forgive them, thus freeing them and ourselves from future emotional ties.

Reincarnation has a tendency to further explain such phenomena as child prodigies, premature death, and genius. How could a man like Edison discover or invent the hundreds of things that he did, when he was not a highly educated scientist? How could Albert Einstein baffle the scientific world with theories that only a handfull of other geniuses could understand, and still develop the atomic bomb *mathematically?* What of the musical ability of a Beethoven or Bach? Could these have been developed in a single lifetime, or was it because the individuals were in fine attunement with Divine Mind?

Concerning premature death, especially by violence, such as war, murder, or suicide, it is generally thought that the entities involved are able to return in a short period of time to continue living among their contemporaries, and to continue their Evolution under situations and societies similar to those they left.

What we call "intuition" or instinct may be a sixth sense, having its origin in either a link with the Super Conscious Mind or a probe into the subconscious levels, bringing forth experiences from the dim past of other lives—a manner of telling us what to do in a given situation, because we have undergone this or a similar event at some earlier time. Personally, I would say that intuition is a combination of 90% contact with Universal Intelligence through our Super Consciousness and 10% subconscious memory.

Many believe that early cave men had such a highly developed intuitive power. Over the centuries we have lost it to a large part, but we still have it to a degree, ready to develop when we acknowledge its presence.

In conclusion, I would like to reiterate that the majority of the world's religions have believed in a form of rebirth, and that it is highly probable that reincarnation was a basic part of the early Christian teachings, as shown by the various biblical references to it, as well as the statements of well known religious leaders of the early centuries.

Reincarnation and other esoteric truths gave way gradually to the easier-to-understand teachings of the early churches with the esoteric teachings replacing them. Reincarnation, as well as other Metaphysical Truths, are not easy to understand without much study, but once they do begin to gradually soak in, they can shed much new light on old writings, and the Bible comes alive with new concepts of Truth.

Whatever reasons may be given for reincarnation, they all add up to the fact that it is the logical method by which the individual reaches God Consciousness. During our many incarnations we are able to gain full awareness of the many facets of life. We are able to experience being men at one time and women at another; we are parents and children, young and old, many times. We must learn, and the sooner the better, to be humble, tolerant, and above all else, to love one another as taught by the great religious leaders of all times.

Today we are doing more soul-searching than ever before, for the Space Age can not allow us to depend on blind faith as our forefathers did, and we find ourselves on the threshold of the greatest religious revival of all time, as we enter the wonderful Age of Spirit.

STRANGE GUESTS BY Brad Steiger
(K-241/50¢)

To carry the Webster definition a step further, a poltergeist is a spirit which gives a form of action to inanimate objects, and which can, as a result of this action, alter the behavior of living things.

Here are but a few of the STRANGE GUESTS who, uninvited and unbidden, have astounded lay observers and trained investigators alike:

- The elusive, talking "thing" that became a family pet
- The fanged poltergeist monster
- The disembodied voice that predicted the future

Authentic stories of inexplicable forces that take possession of places, things, and people.

STRANGE TALENTS BY Bernhardt Hurwood
(K-276/50¢)

Stories of men and women gifted with such rare and weird talents as to astound skeptic and believer alike:

- The living woman who haunted a house
- The doctor who transcended death
- The man whose presence caused spontaneous combustion
- The psychic surgeon who successfully operated without a scapel

These are but four of the 285 factual accounts of seemingly ordinary people with extraordinary abilities to see, hear, and accomplish feats that defy rational explanation.

STRANGE DESTINIES
BY
John Macklin
(K-222/50¢)

For the reader with vision and imagination, here is a fascinating collection of enigmas of life, of science, of fact, guaranteed to challenge the most logical minds—

- The ghost that killed!
- The green-skinned children who walked out of a cave, speaking an unknown language!
- The riddle of the living stones!

Here are baffling accounts that make the reader an eyewitness to the inexplicable.

STRANGE HAPPENINGS
BY
Michael Hervey
(K-259/50¢)

These are Strange Happenings:

- The imaginary man who became a creature of flesh!
- The Berbalang ghouls who inhabit the bodies of men!
- The entire population of a city, who vanished without a trace!

Most of these tales are published here for the first time. Many will become classics of the Strange Facts genre. All will hold the reader's interest from the first page to the last, all of them are true.

THE STRANGE AND UNCANNY

BY

John Macklin

(K-297/50¢)

Here is your validated visa to that mystery-shrouded land inhabited by extraordinary people. Now you can share with them their bone-chilling experiences:

- The man who evoked a demon—that killed him
- The woman who walked into the past
- The cursed ring that haunted Rudolph Valentino

These are but a few of the true mysteries of the world beyond the normal—that strange and fantastic planet that may be waiting for you just around the next bend in the road . . .
